The Brighter Side of Death

The Brighter Side of Death

Tom Holahan

VANTAGE PRESS
New York

Published by Vantage Press, Inc.
419 Park Ave. South, New York, NY 10016

Manufactured in the United States of America
ISBN: 978-0-533-15805-8

Library of Congress Catalog Card No.: 2007903365

0 9 8 7 6 5 4 3 2 1

For all lost souls, adrift on the sea of life, with no direction or destination save death.

Contents

Preface   ix
Introduction   xv

  1. The Journey   1
  2. A Spiritual Autobiography   5
  3. Epiphanies   49
  4. Love   68
  5. Living   89
  6. Success   106
  7. Ethics   133
  8. Politics   146
  9. Religion   156

Conclusion   183

Preface

Professor: Joe, what made you choose a biblical setting?
Joe: You got somethin' against the Bible?
Professor: No, I mean, why did you set your play in Jerusalem, when what you know about is New York? You see every writer, and particularly an inexperienced one, should stick in his own back yard.
Joe: Well, I took lotsa writing courses at NYU nights. Nobody said there was a rule about it.
Professor: Well, there should be. There's no easier way to look ridiculous than by trying to handle something you don't know about.

—Please Don't Eat the Daisies

Joe: Now, if I got you correctly, there's a short stretch of my fiction that you found worthy of note.
Betty: The flashback scene in the courtroom when she tells about being a schoolteacher.
Joe: I *had* a teacher like that once.
Betty: Well, maybe that's why it's good. It's true, it's moving . . .

—Sunset Boulevard

I'm writing this book because I don't know what else to do. I mean, I have plenty of *things* to do, but no vocation. There was a time many years ago when I thought I knew what I wanted to do. Whatever certainty I had then didn't last long, for reasons which I'll explain later. But the feeling, however brief, of having a purpose to my life was so reassuring that I've spent all my subsequent years trying to find another—which could turn out to be writing.

This isn't my first attempt at writing a book. In 1979, after leaving a secure, lucrative job at a blue chip company because I was vaguely discontented, I flew to the west coast with a friend I had met in the Coast Guard. I had no idea what I was going to do. I had sold my house, divested myself of as many worldly possessions as I could foist on my friends and relatives, and resolved to strike out into the great unknown. My original thought in going to California was to check out schools. Possibly, I might study astronomy. In reality, there was an ulterior motive, which was to visit my friend's sister, whom I had met and fallen in love with eight years before. But that's another story. Within two weeks I was back in Rochester, New York, staying with my parents. My attempt to "rekindle" a love that had never burned except in my imagination had failed. After that, I couldn't see any reason to stay in California.

So I moved into a seedy studio apartment on the third floor of a dilapidated old house in what is considered the bohemian section of the city. A lot of young, unattached people live there: aspiring artists, musicians, and assorted free spirits. One day it occurred to me that I could be a writer. I sat down at the typewriter and whipped up a page of history/philosophy/sociology entitled "The Way the World Is," or something like that. Four weeks later I was working for another blue chip company, doing pretty much the same thing as I had done before.

Discontentment, unfortunately, is not so easily disposed of. Within three years, I was on the street again, having left an even better position than I had had with the first company. For the first month I did nothing more than ride my bike a lot and play with my VCRs. Then I got bored. So I occupied myself with consulting work for a few months until the Christmas holidays. By the middle of January I got really bored. On top of that, I had injured my ankle playing tennis. There wasn't much I could do except sit around and read or watch TV. Finally, in desperation, I considered writing again.

Expository and/or creative writing had always been a struggle for me. I dreaded term papers, for example, because of the research involved and the difficulty of finding a way to organize the material. But once I knew what I wanted to say, the actual transferal to paper was relatively easy. The problem was what to write about.

Fortunately, I found an angle. In this I was assisted by a pamphlet I had read a couple of years earlier entitled "STUDIES in the Spirituality of Jesuits: Conversion as a Human Experience," by Paul Robb, S.J. Ever since I had left the Jesuit seminary in 1963, I periodically thought about returning. In connection with this I spoke with former teachers, consulted spiritual advisers, read books, and even tried meditation. My purpose was simply to discern the will of God, figuring that this was the way to true happiness (as Dante put it, "In His will is our peace"[1]). But how do we know what God,

---

[1] *Paradiso,* Canto III, line 85.

assuming He exists, wants us to do? Paul Robb suggested an answer: God speaks to us through the events of our lives.

I had heard somewhere[2] that writers, especially new ones, should write about what they're interested in. There is a strong temptation to write about subjects which the writer thinks the public will like. After all, what's the point of writing if no one else is interested (which translates to: making a living)? On the other hand, what's the point of writing if *you're* not interested?

And so a simple solution presented itself: I would write about my own life, but with the idea of trying to find in it possible clues to my destiny. I would be spared the ordeal of inventing a story and characters. It would be a straight narrative, chronological for the most part, but with ample room for analysis and reflection. It would be an autobiography in the tradition of Thomas Merton's *The Seven Storey Mountain* (my opening paragraph was a thinly disguised imitation of Merton's), the main difference being that he was looking backward from an attained summit, whereas I was looking forward from the midpoint of a journey toward an undetermined destination. My hope was that the book would provide both the reader and myself with some insight into the mystery of human existence. A noble enterprise, indeed. And one that I seemed capable of doing.

And so I wrote: tentatively at first, but then confidently and consistently, until by the end of August I had amassed over 450 single-spaced typewritten pages. I was moderately pleased with what I had written. For the most part, it was a

---

[2] In the movie, *Please Don't Eat the Daisies,* quoted above.

"brain dump." The biggest challenge was to remember: dates, places, people. I tried to tell my story as accurately as possible (though it could have made little difference to the reader whether it was Uncle Joe or Uncle Jim who had given me my first baseball glove). In some cases, I had to reconstruct events based on the memories of other people, though I felt uncomfortable with anything other than my personal recollections. At other times, I reconstructed an event without any memories at all, using only the inference that something like this *must* have happened, or the whole subsequent course of events would have been different. I avoided dialogue except when (a) the event was particularly meaningful and (b) I remembered the exact words spoken. As intended, there was also an abundance of analysis and reflection, which was the kind of writing I enjoyed doing most.

I don't think the book was good enough for publication. It was far from complete and would have required extensive editing. But it was gratifying in one important respect: it proved that I had the discipline and organizational skill to sit down and write a book, as long as the subject interested me. But everything changed in September, when I met a woman who interested me much more than the book. Over the next couple of years, though I managed to add another 300 or so pages to the original manuscript, my interest eventually petered out.

And now, after a succession of jobs, love affairs, and other diversions, I find myself at the age of fifty-nine with nowhere to go and nothing compelling to do. Most people my age are involved with their children and grandchildren, but I have neither of these. It was eight years ago that I met the woman I am now married to (she has four children and five grandchildren). The irony is that this relationship, like my first, occurred with little or no exertion on my part. All the relationships in the intervening thirty-three years, which to a greater or lesser extent were products of my own manufacture, comprise the bulk of my life story.

But for that first love affair, I would probably have become a Jesuit priest. Whether I would have remained so is debatable. After derailing my vocation, Betsy soon departed from my life, leaving me to search the next thirty-three years for a substitute. This search, this *quest,* became at times an obsession. And although it failed, it did provide me with the raw materials for this book—and maybe others.

Introduction

Rosalyn: But what if he died? It would be terrible.
Gay: Honey, we all gotta go sometime, reason or no
           reason. Dyin's as natural as livin'. A man who's
           too afraid to die is too afraid to live.

                                        — *The Misfits*

Contrary to what the title might suggest, this is *not* a book about suicide.

It's really a book about life (the meaning of). The title is meant to grab the reader's attention by making an assertion that runs counter to the current ethos, which has been variously stated as:

- You only go round once in life, so go for all the gusto you can.
- Be all that you can be.
- He who dies with the most toys wins. (Etc.)

What is the meaning (or purpose) of life?
This is really two questions:

1. What is the meaning of life in general?
2. What is the meaning of *my* life?

These questions have proven so intractable over the centuries that I believe many people (if not most) have stopped asking them. And I think there is justification for not asking: after all, if history's most intelligent, most spiritual, most insightful men and women have not been able to provide definitive and satisfying answers, at least to the satisfaction of a moderate skeptic, then maybe they're beyond reach. In which case, it might be better to occupy ourselves with more practical pursuits.

Many people reach this conclusion at an early age. They sense that the search for some ultimate purpose to life would be futile, so they decide (probably not consciously) on either or both of two basic courses of action:

1. Shelve the question entirely and focus on real, material issues, such as food, clothing, sex, money, success, knowledge, etc.
2. Accept the teachings of an organized religion, as to ultimate causes and purposes, and conduct oneself within its ethical boundaries.

I admit, up front, that I have not found a definitive answer to either of the above questions. I had hoped that, after the research and reflection which the writing of this book entailed, I would be closer to the answers. And I believe I am. But I'm still not completely satisfied.

However, *we shouldn't stop asking a question simply because a definitive answer appears to be unattainable.* This is one of the fundamental points I wish to make. The search for an answer still has value, even if the only result is a better restatement of the question.

So what does finding the meaning of life have to do with the title of this book?

I believe there are five pathways to finding the meaning of life:

1. Mysticism (meditation or contemplative prayer)
2. An epiphany
3. Self-examination
4. Observation and reflection
5. Death

Let me say a few words about each. After reading my thoughts on death, I think the reader will see the connection.

Mysticism

Mysticism is a subject about which I profess to know very little. At various times in my life I have tried meditation as a way to discern the will of God (or, more accurately, to obtain ratification for a course already decided on); but my attempts were half-hearted, at best. I couldn't shake my suspicion that the human mind had an almost infinite capacity for deluding itself. Was it God the mystics had experienced or merely

an undigested bit of beef, a piece of cheese, a fragment of underdone potato . . . ?

—*Scrooge*

Like most hyperactive Americans of the 20th or 21st century, I found it almost impossible (or even desirable) to sit quietly in semi-darkness without falling asleep. Which brings to mind a fond memory:

When I was in the Jesuit seminary, in the summer and fall of 1963, there were two daily meditation periods: 6 to 7 A.M. and 5:30 to 6 P.M. Human nature being what it is, the rule was that one member of our group would be assigned the job (for the whole week, both morning and afternoon) of doing the *visitatio*.[1] This consisted of stealthily opening the door to each person's room, at some randomly chosen time during the meditation period, and checking the condition of the occupant. As you can imagine, the occupants would be in various positions: from kneeling at the prie-dieu, to leaning against the wall, to sleeping on the bed. We were never told what to do if we found someone in a less than optimum prayer position. I guess the possible opprobrium of one's peer was thought to be motivation enough to stay awake.

As with most things at that time in my life, I struggled mightily to master the art of contemplative prayer. And, as usual, I succeeded in form, if not in substance. I would try again two or three other times later in life, but only because my spiritual director encouraged it. For the present at least, I've given up on meditation as a gateway to ultimate meaning. However, I accept the legitimacy of mystics such as Thomas Merton, whose testimony[2] has the ring of truth.

Which brings me to the second pathway: an epiphany.

---

[1] Latin for *visit.*
[2] Cf. *The Seven Storey Mountain.*

Epiphany

The word *epiphany* (capital *E*) refers to the Christian feast of January 6th commemorating the manifestation of the infant Christ to the gentiles (represented by the Magi or Three Kings). James Joyce used the word in the sense that I will be using it here: a moment of sudden intuitive understanding or flash of insight. In other words, it's as if the sky or the earth were suddenly opened and you could see directly into eternity. That experience, though brief, would be so intense that it would be capable of stirring profound emotion for the rest of one's life.

Unfortunately, epiphanies are rare, if they occur at all. Also, they seem to occur at random, with no advance notice. There are two experiences in my own life I would characterize as epiphanies (to be discussed later in the chapter entitled "Epiphanies"); but, of course, such labeling is highly subjective. At any rate, since epiphanies by definition can't be induced or anticipated, they are not a reliable pathway to meaning.

Self-Examination

The idea of using self-examination as a pathway to meaning consists of reviewing the events of one's life and trying to discern patterns in the past which might suggest possibilities for future action, study, or reflection. This was first suggested to me by a pamphlet entitled "STUDIES in the Spirituality of Jesuits: Conversion As a Human Experience," by Paul Robb, S.J., which I read in 1980 during an intense period of listlessness and confusion. At the time, I was trying to decide whether to return to the seminary. One of my spiritual directors recommended this pamphlet as an aid to discernment, which is the process of determining God's will for each of us.

Since much of the remainder of this book is devoted to the results of my self-examination, I won't say anything more about it here.

Observation and Reflection

Observation and reflection is the process of analyzing the data of life, both past and present. Here, the emphasis is on external, objective events; i.e., events outside oneself. While self-examination may be more useful in answering the second of the two ultimate questions (What is the meaning of *my* life?), observation and reflection may be more useful for answering the first (What is the meaning of life in general?).

Observation and reflection also comprise a significant portion of this book and therefore will be left to the subsequent chapters.

That leaves us with the final[3] pathway: death.

---

[3] In more ways than one.

Death

Death is a subject we would rather not talk about. We spend a goodly portion of our lives trying to deny it, postpone it, or prevent it altogether.

However, Christianity (at least the Catholic version which I grew up with) has a radically different view. Death is seen as a desirable thing, a way of escaping this earthly vale of tears and being united with God. Mortal life is not viewed as an end in itself but as a preparation for eternal life. This idea was drummed relentlessly into my head, from first grade through college: how we conducted ourselves here, on earth and in time, would determine how (and where) we would spend eternity.

But Christianity, like everything else, has been tainted by the prevailing zeitgeist, which has been called *secular humanism*: the view that man is the measure of all things, the material world is all there is, and therefore get all you can out of your earthly existence ("go for the gusto," etc.).

Which all makes perfect sense if you don't concede the existence of anything but sensate reality.

This conflicts with the central theme of Christianity, which is the Resurrection: death is not the end of life, but the beginning. In the words of Dylan Thomas (*A Refusal to Mourn the Death, by Fire, of a Child in London*): "After the first death, there is no other."[4] If death could be as quick and clean as flipping a light switch, then it might be worth trying. At least we would find out whether the Christian message is true

---

[4] Dylan Thomas, *Collected Poems* (New York, New Directions Publishing Corporation, 1957), p. 112.

or not. Of course, if it turns out that death is the end of every-thing, then we won't know the truth of this or anything else.

With the exception of mysticism, which I have decided to ignore, and death, which I have not yet experienced, all of the above pathways will be employed in this book. The dis-cussion of epiphanies as a pathway to meaning will be con-fined to its own chapter. Aside from that, the remaining two pathways (self-examination and observation/reflection) will provide the guiding methodology for the rest of the book. While I believe that these two pathways can produce much useful information and insight, I still think that only death will yield the definitive answers to the fundamental ques-tions. Hence, the book's title.

Unfortunately, however, if I were to take that pathway, I wouldn't be able to write about it.

My basic problem is this (which is the driving force behind this book): why did God create such a magnificent universe, full of possibility and promise, and then devalue it, as Christ seems to do in the Gospels, particularly in *The Gospel of Saint Mark*? I find it difficult to believe that God created the universe merely as a testing ground, where human beings could prove whether or not they were worthy to enter the Kingdom. In addition, with my advancing age and awareness of just how flawed Man[5] is, I wonder how God could entrust him[6] with the overwhelming re-

---

[5] The term "Man" in this context is used to mean "mankind" or "the human race," not a male person.

[6] In accordance with traditional grammar, I use the masculine pronoun to repre-sent human beings of both sexes.

sponsibility of settling his own fate for eternity. It would seem that Man, by design, is not up to the task.

To me, this is the fundamental paradox of Christianity: the world (what we perceive) versus the Kingdom of God (the spiritual life, eternity)—what *should* we do in the here and now? Does it matter whether we achieve peace in the Middle East? Or whether Johnny goes to medical school? Or whether Uncle Joe takes his blood pressure pills? Does any of this mean anything in the context of eternity?

I invite the reader to come with me on a quest to answer these questions—and many others—always mindful of the two basic questions posed at the start. Structurally, the book is divided into chapters, each of which is devoted to a major theme:

1. The Journey
2. A Spiritual Autobiography
3. Epiphanies
4. Love
5. Living
6. Success
7. Ethics
8. Politics
9. Religion
   Conclusion

The chapters are further divided into subsections, which explore various aspects of each theme. Each chapter begins with a favorite movie quote,[7] hopefully apropos of the sub-

---

[7] Someone once said that the answers to all life's questions can be found in the movies.

ject at hand. Actually, movie quotes, as well as quotations from other sources, are liable to appear anywhere. Writers need all the help they can get.

The Brighter Side of Death

1. The Journey

Fr. Pero: You are still by, by the world's standards, a youngish man. Yet, in the normal course of existence, you can expect 20 or 30 years of gradually diminishing activity. Here, however, in Shangri-La, your life has just begun and may go on and on.

Conway: To be candid, Father, a prolonged future doesn't excite me. It would have to have a point. I've sometimes doubted whether life itself has any. If that is so, then long life must be even more pointless. No, I'd need a much more definite reason for going on and on.

—Lost Horizon

Life is a mystery. By life, I mean existence, *being,* which includes everything that is: the universe (objects) and ourselves (subjects).

We know very little of significance about either. Over the centuries, we have accumulated a lot of information. We even have a pretty good idea of how the universe works, both on the microscopic[1] and macroscopic[2] levels.

---

[1] I.e., atomic, described by the Quantum Theory.

[2] I.e., cosmic, described by the General Theory of Relativity.

But the answers to the fundamental questions, who (or what) and why, continue to elude us.

Who (or what) caused the universe? Did God create it, or was it the result of a quantum fluctuation? Perhaps the universe is eternal and therefore uncreated. Theories abound, but it's doubtful we'll get a definitive answer, at least using the methodology of science.

The *why* question is even more problematical. Scientists state flatly that they don't deal in *why* questions (in the sense of meaning or purpose). This has been left traditionally in the hands of philosophers and theologians. But they haven't been much help either. It seems to me that philosophers spend most of their time arguing about the structure of language (to the neglect of metaphysics, the study of *being*), while theologians are preoccupied with deciphering ancient texts and then trying to assemble their confusing and often contradictory statements into a coherent message.

Either way, we're left in doubt. The mystery remains.

Instinctively, most people realize this. They accept the fact that they're not going to get definitive answers to the fundamental questions; and, understandably, they move on. The alternative would be to confront the Abyss, which is far too frightening a prospect for all but the most philosophically inquisitive.

And so life becomes a vast conspiracy of diversions: activities designed to mask the face of Nothingness. Chief among these is family, which then spawns a host of ancillary pursuits: job, money, recreation, education, and even religion (as a buttress to the whole enterprise). For those not involved in the family game, the situation is somewhat more difficult: how to justify and give meaning to one's life merely on the basis of self-fulfillment. This may involve a "noble" occupation, such as ministry or medicine, or it may simply be the pursuit of pleasure.

However, I submit that the quest for fundamental answers is worthwhile, even though the chance for success may be nil. Who knows? Something may turn up along the way. Christ said, "Seek and you shall find."[3] In the *Apology*, Socrates said:

> Perhaps someone may say, But surely, Socrates, after you have left us [i.e., in exile] you can spend the rest of your life in quietly minding your own business.
>
> This is the hardest thing of all to make some of you understand. If I say that this would be disobedience to God, and that is why I cannot "mind my own business," you will not believe that I am serious. If on the other hand I tell you that to let no day pass without discussing goodness and all the other subjects about which you hear me talking and examining both myself and others is really the very best thing that a man can do, and that life without this sort of examination is not worth living, you will be even less inclined to believe me.[4]

On the other hand, people who go looking for something generally find it, whether it's there or not. And herein lies the dilemma: the desire for wisdom, a fundamental understanding of the meaning and purpose of existence, beck-

---

[3] Matthew 7:7.

[4] *The Collected Dialogues of Plato*, ed. By Edith Hamilton and Huntington Cairns (Princeton, Princeton University Press, 1989), pp. 22–23.

ons us toward an unknown territory, where signposts are few and the compass is useless, where false guides and gods may mislead us, and where death may be the only gateway to certainty. But not to make the journey would be unthinkable—a kind of intellectual and moral suicide.

I have undertaken such a journey. I am still en route, not sure of where I am or where I'm going. What follows is an attempt to map where I have been so far.

2. A Spiritual Autobiography

Nan:	Well . . . what do you believe in?
Alec:	[Laughs]
Nan:	Well, don't laugh. Tell me.
Alec:	Well, I believe that a No. 11 bus will get me to Hammersmith—I do not believe it will be driven by . . . uh . . . Father Christmas.

—The Spy Who Came In from the Cold

Background

I grew up in an environment as religious as any in America.

It's hard for young people today to imagine what it was like in the early 1950s. It was a time of material prosperity, at least compared to the Great Depression of the 1930s, which was still very fresh in the minds of my parents' generation. Even my family, which would have been considered lower middle class, never wanted for the basics: food, clothing, a decent place to live, and even a few frills (in my case: toys or an occasional outing somewhere, usually the ballpark).

The big difference between the 1950s and the present is what is currently referred to as the "culture" (as in *culture wars*), which I will define as the underlying moral and religious assumptions of society. In the 1950s, the churches were

5

stronger. People took the practice of their religion much more seriously; consequently, the three major American faiths (Protestantism, Catholicism, and Judaism) had a much stronger identity. Remember, this was before the ecumenical movement. If you were born a Catholic, you stayed a Catholic. In fact, you were discouraged from even associating with people of other faiths. I'm sure this was one of the main reasons why Catholics had their own school system. The overwhelming majority of Catholics sent their children to Catholic schools, at least until eighth grade.

I was raised a Catholic. I remember the nuns telling us that people of other faiths, though not necessarily evil, were in some sense deficient. Perhaps they were just unlucky not to have been born into the "true faith," in which case it was our duty to enlighten them. One of my early teachers must have been a bit overzealous (or maybe I was too impressionable—or both), because I caused my parents some embarrassment one day when we were riding in the car with their friends. I made an offhand remark about "those dirty Protestants," not realizing that Mr. and Mrs. Potter were Presbyterians. In fact, Mr. Potter had been in the ministry before starting his heating and cooling business. Of course, nothing was said to me at the time of the remark; but I'm sure my parents explained to me later that even though the Potters were not Catholics, they were still good people and that I should never say anything like that again. Even in those days of strong religious identity, people at least had common sense.

However, just because people in the 1950s had powerful ties to specific faiths, it does not mean that they didn't agree on basic moral and religious principles. For example, almost everybody believed that there was a God, that there was an afterlife, and that one's actions in this life determined what that afterlife would be. There was also general acceptance of the Bible, especially the Ten Commandments, as a moral guide. Premarital sex was considered taboo, as was extramarital sex and divorce. Profanity was unacceptable and was never used in any environment where I happened to be. Even words like "pregnant" were seldom used and only with great discretion.

It's instructive to compare the television programming of the 1950s with that of today. I remember the big stir caused by the decision to incorporate Lucille Ball's real-life pregnancy into the *I Love Lucy* show in 1952. And then, of course, there were the twin beds, which appeared in all the sitcoms of the 1950s. Sex was never an acceptable theme. Marriage was, but only in the safe, traditional ways (e.g., mother-in-law problems, shopping excesses, male/female foibles, etc.). Flirtations, or even the suggestion of an extramarital involvement, were sanitized and rendered harmless—often explained as an innocent misunderstanding, as in the screwball comedies of the 1930s.

At any rate, I think it's safe to say that in the 1950s, there was general agreement about the fundamentals of religion and morality. There would have been no problem with the phrase "under God" in the Pledge of Allegiance or the banning of sex education, let alone condom distribution, in the public schools.

Religious Education

My religious education was strict, intense, and thor-

7

ough. This was in large part due to the fact that *all* of my elementary school teachers were nuns and more than half of my high school and college teachers were Jesuit scholastics[1] and priests. I can still quote from memory one of the questions from the *Baltimore Catechism* (the basic religious textbook used in all Catholic elementary schools in the 1950s):

Q: Why did God make us?
A: To know, love, and serve Him in this world and be happy with Him in the next.

In those days, for a Catholic boy or girl, being a priest or a nun was considered to be the highest career one could aspire to. There was a special name for it: *vocation,* which means a calling by God.

As for me, I gave no more than a passing thought to the idea of becoming a priest. My ambition was to become a major league ball player, like my heroes Stan Musial, Ted Williams, and Joe DiMaggio. My dad and my Uncle Ted, who were both excellent ball players, taught me the basics; and I learned the rest on the neighborhood playgrounds. However, by the end of 8th grade it became clear to me that a career in professional baseball was not in the cards. Dad, who had recently got a job with the local power company, encouraged me to consider electrical engineering.

I had been an outstanding student all through grammar school. My 8th grade teacher, a strict, conservative old nun who referred to cars as "machines," pushed me toward

---

[1] A scholastic is a member of a religious order who is studying to become a priest.

8

McQuaid, the top Catholic high school in the area. I was reluctant at first, not having taken academics too seriously despite my good marks. But one of my best friends was going there; so I decided to give it a try.

I entered McQuaid in the fall of 1959 with two things in mind: a career in electrical engineering and a determination not to work too hard to achieve it. But I hadn't counted on the influence of the Jesuits, the Society of Jesus, who ran the school. A more amazing group of men could not be found.[2] In one sense, they could be described as the spiritual shock troops of the Catholic Church. St. Ignatius Loyola, founder of the Jesuits, had been a military officer before his conversion to the service of God. Indeed, when I was in the Coast Guard, I noticed many parallels between the military and the Jesuits. Most of the Jesuits I encountered at McQuaid were tough and strict.

But there were other aspects of the Jesuits, too. For example, they were learned men. They all had at least a Master's Degree in their chosen field. Many would go on to doctorates at the most prestigious universities in the world. They demanded—and got—academic excellence from their students.

However, the thing I admired most about the Jesuits was their openness to facts and ideas that might run counter to orthodox Catholic thinking. Many Catholics were afraid of be-

---

[2] Apparently *Time* Magazine thought so, too. In the early 1980s, *Time* ran a cover story which showed the remarkable diversity of talents, philosophies, and interests among the Society's members. In addition to being priests, which of course was their primary role, they were also scientists, doctors, lawyers, political activists, congressmen, presidential speech writers, actors, and clowns.

ing tainted by the prevailing secular philosophy. Their idea of education was to use it as a defense against the onslaught of a pagan world. Science, philosophy, history, etc. were all to be shaped by the Catholic worldview.

The Jesuit approach was different. Secure in their religious faith, the Jesuits feared nothing. Consequently, neither did we. All of reality was subject to rational inquiry. Conclusions were to be based on fact, not on preconceived notions of philosophy and theology.

Vocation

Despite a casual approach to study and a more challenging curriculum, I completed my first year at McQuaid with a 90+ average. I was beginning to fall under the Jesuit spell, mostly due to my Latin and English teachers; but my basic attitude was unchanged. The proof of this was in my refusal to enter the Advanced Placement in English (APE) program, which was to begin in sophomore year. The reason: a summer reading list and the prospect of additional work during the upcoming year. Besides, what did this have to do with electrical engineering, which was still my nominal career goal?

A year later I was kicking myself.

The turning point came in October. Our new homeroom teacher, who also taught Latin, Religion/Guidance, and APE, bore some resemblance to the Jesuits I had had the year before, except that he was even stricter and tougher. It soon became obvious to me that I couldn't get away with doing my Latin homework on the bus ride home, as I had routinely done in my freshman year. This new teacher was much more aggressive. He wouldn't just call on people who raised their hands; he would call on anyone at any time. If you failed to give the correct answer, he would stare at you icily, sometimes adding a sarcastic remark that made you feel horrible. The first time this happened to me, I was determined never to let it happen again.

My study habits were completely transformed.

In his role as Guidance Counselor, Vince Duminuco taught us how to study. The first thing was to have a quiet place, preferably a separate room, far removed from any distractions, such as radio, TV, etc. Second, you had to have a desk with nothing on it but a good reading lamp. The only other things permitted on that desk were the materials for the subject at hand: paper, pen, textbook. The third requirement was a schedule of subjects: hardest first, easiest, next hardest, next easiest, etc., with a ten-minute break after each subject. Under no circumstances were you to watch television until *all* your homework was done. This created a problem for me because I was still somewhat addicted to television. For example, on Tuesday night *Peter Gunn* started at 9 P.M. This meant that I had to have all my homework done by 9. To do this, I had to get my hardest subject (Latin, Geometry, or Greek) done before dinner, which was usually around 5:30. I had given up trying to do any homework on the bus for two reasons: my new study routine prohibited it and I started noticing the girls who rode on the bus.

Vince Duminuco also encouraged his students not to rush home after school, but to stay around and participate in one of the many extracurricular activities, such as band, dramatics, sports, etc. He felt that it was not enough to be successful in academics. In order to be well-rounded, you needed to be involved in some sort of outside activity. For me, this was TV during the school week and hanging around with my neighborhood friends on the weekend. I didn't want anything to interfere with my newly acquired study routine.

In truth, I became a slave to my study schedule. I was so fanatical that I wouldn't let anything interfere with it. Originally, my intent was to make sure that I finished studying in time to enjoy my favorite TV shows. But as time went on, adherence to the schedule became an end in itself, even to the point where the TV shows didn't matter any more. I found myself doing homework four or five hours a night. This provided my main source of satisfaction, much as an athlete finds satisfaction in a rigorous training schedule, knowing that it will provide him with an edge in competition. And so my study routine provided me with an edge in the classroom, particularly Vince Duminuco's Latin class, where I felt confident that I could answer any question thrown at me. I felt positively elated when Vince indicated his approval with a smile or compliment. It was now that I began to regret not signing up for Vince's APE class. Every day at 1 P.M. I'd go next door to the alternate English class, taught by a charming but obviously troubled Jesuit scholastic. Upon returning, I would notice tantalizing words and phrases on the blackboard, indicative of a far more stimulating class than the one I'd just been in.

Vince was the most influential teacher of my life. He instilled discipline, love of excellence, and intellectual passion. But at the end of sophomore year, my career goal was the same as it had been at the start of high school: electrical engineering.

The interesting thing was that I was on the wrong academic track for my professed career. Honors Program students, of which I was one, had two options: Science Honors and Greek Honors. For some reason, at the end of freshman year, I had chosen Greek Honors. Perhaps this was due to the influence of one of my two Jesuit teachers. Jesuits, generally, seem to prefer the humanities to the sciences. This may also be indicative of the fact that my career orientation was not very strong: my thoughts of life beyond high school were still pretty vague.

Junior year turned out to be the pivotal year, despite the fact that I had no single outstanding teacher, like Vince the year before. The key was a book, *The Ugly American,* which I don't think was even connected with any of my classes (in those days, I didn't do much outside reading). The book painted a bleak picture of American diplomacy in the postwar years, particularly as it related to Southeast Asia, which was soon to explode into the Vietnam War. I decided then and there that I would devote my considerable language skills (I had just begun my third foreign language, Russian, at the beginning of junior year) to the Foreign Service. Perhaps not coincidentally, I noted that Georgetown University, a Jesuit institution, had a school of Foreign Service. Later, as the New Frontier gained momentum, my thoughts turned to the Peace Corps. Conspicuously absent were any thoughts of love and marriage, except in that general idealized form which we all fantasize about.

And so, as I approached my final year of high school, I was definitely decided upon some sort of career in public service, probably the Peace Corps or something related to it. Suddenly, shortly after I returned to school from summer vacation, it occurred to me that I should become a Jesuit priest. I don't know whether this idea had been simmering inside of me for a long time or whether it was a kind of Joycean epiphany. (No, this was not one of the two possible epiphanies referred to in the Introduction.) Upon careful consideration, it made perfect sense. Not only did it coincide with my growing desire to serve humanity in the most profound way (spiritually), but it also sidestepped an issue which was becoming increasingly problematical: sex.

All through sophomore and junior year I was becoming increasingly fascinated with girls. I'd see them on the bus, both morning and evening, and dream about what it would be like to be with them. It was not sexual desire (I had no idea what that meant), but more a mixture of curiosity and admiration, like looking at a brand new car. Up to this point, I had experienced my own sexuality only as a confused and uncomfortable series of erections and wet dreams. The whole idea of sex, while potentially exciting, seemed messy and embarrassing. In short, I was afraid of the whole prospect. The Catholic priesthood, which prohibited marriage for its members, seemed like a good way out.

This, of course, is how it looks in retrospect. At the time, I didn't reason things out in the calculated way described above. But the decision to enter the Jesuit priesthood did come as sort of a relief, because even though I was attracted to girls, I sensed that love and marriage were too complicated for my taste. I have always wanted things to be simple; relationships with other human beings, especially close ones, are seldom that.

First Love

As of September, 1962, I had never had a date with a girl. At this point, I didn't want one. I had just made up my mind to apply for admission to the Jesuits, and I didn't want any complications or distractions. Then, one of those things occurred which make you believe that there may be a supernatural[3] aspect to human existence after all. Out of the blue I received a phone call from a girl asking me to a dance.

I was completely taken aback. This was totally unexpected; and to make matters worse, I didn't know who she was. After a few seconds, I realized that we had two points of connection. First, I had seen her a few times the summer before last, when she accompanied our baseball coach to babysit for his toddler son. More recently, I had seen her in church. Since early September, I had started attending daily Mass at the neighborhood church. This was not the church I normally attended, but it was close enough so that I could walk there and back before the bus came to pick me up for school. It seems that her family was also very religious and that she made it a habit to attend daily Mass, even though she had no interest in becoming a nun. This phone conversation was the first time we had ever spoken to each other.

Why do I attach supernatural significance to this rather mundane event? Because it changed the whole course of my life. If Betsy hadn't called that evening, chances are I would have become a Jesuit priest. Whether I would have remained

---

[3] In the sense that each of us has a destiny, prearranged for us by God.

one is less certain; but I wouldn't have left the seminary when I did.

In retrospect, I'm surprised that I accepted Betsy's invitation. As I spoke to her that evening, I didn't have a clear picture of what she looked like. I had never seen her up close; or, if I had, I must not have paid too much attention. I had a vague notion that she was cute, so I wasn't about to refuse her on that basis (I had been invited to a junior prom the year before by a girl I had gone to grammar school with, but I declined her invitation because I wasn't attracted to her). I told Betsy that I didn't know how to dance, still trying to decide whether I wanted to go with her. I think she was about to end the conversation, probably convinced that I didn't want to go, when I impulsively suggested that she could teach me how to dance before we went! I don't know what made me say that. I must have thought that going to the dance would be good for me, in terms of social development (I had not attended a social event of any kind since eighth grade, when one of the girls in the class had a Halloween Party at her house).

A week before the actual dance, we agreed to meet at her house for dance lessons. As it turned out, we spent the entire evening talking with her parents and one of their friends. Even though I was terrified at the prospect of not knowing how to dance, I at least was glad to be going with Betsy. She was indeed cute, easy to talk to, and we had a good time. I hadn't fallen in love with her yet. I was merely looking forward to having a good time at the dance. My vocation was still secure.

A week later, everything changed. It was Friday, October 19, 1962. The Cuban Missile Crisis was still on everyone's mind as Betsy and her parents pulled into our driveway

16

to pick me up. Even though Betsy and I had driver's licenses, we weren't old enough to drive after sunset.[4] Since it was Betsy's dance, and I wasn't old enough to take her by myself, Betsy's parents had to provide the transportation, which is probably why they volunteered to be chaperones, since they had to go there anyway. Being late October, it was already dark. I didn't get a good look at Betsy when I climbed into the back seat with her, but I immediately sensed that this was going to be a special evening. Even in the dim light of the car, I could see that she was different. When we arrived at the dance and I saw her in the full light of the festive hall, I immediately fell in love. Gone were the schoolgirl frocks, bobby socks, and saddle shoes. Here was a beautiful young woman, complete with makeup, dress, stockings, and high heels. I was excited and terrified at the same time.

I woke up the next morning with an awful dilemma. The previous evening had been the most wonderful in my life, but what was I going to do now? I had already made my intentions known concerning the Jesuits. But I wasn't thinking about the Jesuits any more. I couldn't think of anything except Betsy. Despite being hopelessly and totally in love, I was confronted by the brutal fact that I was woefully naïve about sex. I didn't know the mechanics of sex, and I didn't know the psychology of sex. Certainly, I wanted to pursue a relationship with Betsy; but I had no idea of how to go about it. I would have no problem asking her for a date, since I

---

[4] In New York State, you had to be 18 to drive alone (i.e., without an 18-year old license holder in the car) after dark or 17 if you had passed a driver education course.

knew that she liked me, at least as a friend; but then what? After an unspecified time, I assumed that you were expected to get physical. I had never kissed a woman before, other than my female relatives, and these had not been lover's kisses. After a few days of this sort of thinking, I decided that a love affair with Betsy or any other woman was out of the question.

Shortly after this, I told Betsy that I intended to become a Jesuit. This had the effect of protecting me from her, while at the same time making us closer. I think she was flattered by the fact that I took her into my confidence. I also think that she was a little saddened by my admission, possibly because she had romantic intentions toward me. But, being a good Catholic girl, she must have admired and respected me for wanting to become a priest. Perhaps, without realizing it, I had fashioned a strategy: to postpone any final decision regarding romantic involvement with Betsy but also to enhance her opinion of me.

As things turned out, we remained friends for the rest of that year. We went on several dates, as friends, mostly to fulfill social obligations which required a person of the opposite sex. However, unbeknownst to me, she had irrevocably decided against me as a lover. I, on the other hand, was still in love with her; and I assumed that she would be available to me if and when my career as a Jesuit was over.

The Seminary

I, along with three of my classmates from McQuaid, arrived at Bellarmine College on July 30, 1963. Situated on the west shore of Lake Champlain about 5 miles south of the city of Plattsburgh, New York, Bellarmine was the seminary for the Buffalo Province of the Society of Jesus. The building, which resembled an old colonial mansion, was a massive structure, made of stucco and brick. In its heyday, it was known as the *Hotel Champlain,* one of the poshest resorts in upstate New York. Recently, it had fallen on hard times and been forced to close. The Jesuits, having split the New York Province into two smaller ones,[5] needed another novitiate.[6] So for a bargain basement price they picked up the *Hotel Champlain,* formerly a playground for the rich and famous, and turned it into a training camp for future priests and brothers.

For the most part, the *Hotel Champlain,* renamed Bellarmine College after St. Robert Bellarmine, was ideally suited for its mission. It was pastorally serene, isolated, and set up for the occupation of a large number of individuals, along with all the supporting functions: chapel (which obviously had been converted from something else), kitchen, dining hall, laundry, etc. The large common rooms were all on the first floor, with the residence rooms and suites on the second through fifth floors. The largest of these, which were reserved for the administrators and faculty, were on the second floor, with the rooms diminishing in size as you went higher. Rooms were assigned on the basis of seniority. The pecking order was: second-year juniors (college sophomores), first-year juniors (college freshmen), second-year novices

---

[5] The Buffalo Province comprised upstate New York, which was everything north and west of Newburg, while the New York Province included the greater New York City area and part of New Jersey.

[6] A novitiate is a seminary for the first 2 years of Jesuit training.

(*secundi*), and first-year novices (*primi*). Being new, we were given small, single rooms on the fifth floor (with communal showers at the end of the hall).

The only drawbacks to Bellarmine were the high cost of maintaining the antiquated plumbing and heating systems and the fact that just across the highway was Plattsburgh Air Force Base, part of the Strategic Air Command (SAC). This meant that there was almost a constant whine of jet engines, both day and night. If you were unlucky to have a room facing the air base, you could be kept awake by the brilliant landing lights and the comings and goings of B-52 and B-58 bombers. The construction of this air base, which occurred after World War II, might have been partly responsible for the demise of the *Hotel Champlain*. After all, who would want to spend their vacation next to a SAC base?

Anyway, I arrived at Bellarmine under a cloud. Betsy was constantly on my mind, but I hadn't yet devised an exit strategy. I was determined, for the time being at least, to stick it out. Perhaps something would happen to make things easier, like forgetting Betsy or becoming totally engrossed in the process of becoming a Jesuit.

Spiritually, I was inept. This was normal for a Catholic at that time. We had been taught (perhaps "indoctrinated" is a better word) to accept the teachings of the Church without question. The *Baltimore Catechism* had been drummed into our heads since first grade. Jesuit religious instruction in high school was somewhat more sophisticated but essentially the same. However, by their actions and offhand remarks, the Jesuits suggested that there might be some leeway in the rigorous and uncompromising teachings of the Church. As far as prayer was concerned, the emphasis was on using the traditional and formulaic, such as the *Our Father* and the *Hail Mary*. The idea of prayer as actual communication with God was not promulgated.

This was about to change.

Seminary comes from the Latin word *semen* (seed). It is an institution for the training of priests, where the seed of spiritual life may grow and prosper. The focus is on theology and related courses, although some attention may be given to spiritual development, as in learning and practicing methods of prayer. A novitiate is a special type of seminary which is devoted exclusively to the spiritual formation of members of a religious order, such as the Jesuits, Franciscans, Dominicans, etc. In our case, we received a daily dose of Latin, just to keep up our academic skills. At that time, Latin was still the official language of the Catholic Church. Use of the vernacular (English) in Church functions, though approved by the Second Vatican Council, had not yet filtered down to the general public, though we occasionally had English Masses at Bellarmine. In fact, Latin was technically the language of communication within the novitiate, which meant that we were supposed to use it when talking to each other or the faculty. However, as mentioned earlier, the emphasis was on spiritual development, which included an hour of meditation (also known as contemplative prayer) in the morning, another half hour in the afternoon, and classroom sessions devoted to mastering the techniques of meditation.

All this was under the direct supervision of the Master of Novices, a combination drill sergeant, father confessor, teacher, and Dutch uncle. His name was Jim Demske. After serving in the U.S. Army in World War II, he entered the Jesuits. He became one of the leading authorities on the philosophy of Martin Heidegger, with whom he had studied in Germany. In the normal course of events, he should have taken up residence as a philosophy professor at a prestigious university. Instead, he was assigned as wet nurse to a bunch of teenagers.[7] Whether intended or not, it turned out to be a lesson in humility and obedience for Jim, who never gave us any indication that the job of Novice Master was beneath his dignity. In fact, I can't imagine anyone doing a better job. Jim's lack of formal training for his assignment was actually an advantage, since he came to it with an open mind and a willingness to try new approaches to things. For example, one of the first things he did was to eliminate the "talk Latin" rule. Of course, talking of any kind was forbidden most of the time; but at least you could speak in your native tongue when permitted (as at meals, when you wanted someone to pass something to you). Another was to discourage the practice of self-inflicted medieval torture, as in the use of the flag and the chain. The flag (short for the Latin *flagellum*) was a miniature cat-o-nine-tails which you could beat yourself with during penitential periods, such as the Long Retreat or Lent. The chain (Latin: *catena*) was a barbaric device with little barbs formed in the links. The idea was to wrap this thing around your leg or arm tightly enough so that the barbs would penetrate (or at least bruise) the flesh as you moved about. In other words, you would wear it like a garter for as long as you could stand it.

Jim brought a practical approach to the business of mak-

---

[7] Most of us were just out of high school. A few had completed some college. One or two had Bachelors Degrees and one guy had a doctorate in chemistry.

ing Jesuits. Previously, things had been done by tradition, without any thought to their utility. Jim's attitude was: if a thing didn't make sense, get rid of it. And he did. Unfortunately for me, I didn't stay around long enough to take advantage of my association with this remarkable man.

I started out with good intentions, but my heart just wasn't in it. If it weren't for Betsy, I probably would have remained in the Jesuits. Although I was homesick for the usual reasons (family, friends, activities), I don't think that this would have caused me to leave. Basically, it wasn't a bad life. I didn't mind the deprivations: TV and soda pop were the things I missed most. The isolation and the lack of a social life didn't bother me, since my closest friend was in the seminary with me. The regimented schedule kept us busy. The worst parts of the day for me were the two meditation periods: 6 to 7 in the morning and 5:30 to 6 in the afternoon. It was during these times, when we were supposed to be meditating about the mystery and majesty of Jesus Christ, that I found it most difficult to keep my mind off Betsy. To a certain extent, I felt guilty because I wasn't doing what I should have been doing. In all other respects, though, I think I did my duty. As the days passed, however, I wondered whether I could keep my sanity.

Finally, a significant event occurred. We had our first spiritual casualty: one of my fellow novices called it quits. It happened during the second week of the Long Retreat, a thirty-day period of intense spiritual activity, centered in the *Spiritual Exercises of St. Ignatius.* Jesuits make many retreats during the course of their careers, but the Long Retreat is only prescribed twice: during the first year of novitiate and during the last year of formal training, called tertianship, which would have occurred in my fifteenth year, had I stayed. In hindsight, I look upon the Long Retreat as a kind of initiation, similar to basic training in the military, which is designed to weed out those who can't take it. This is perhaps too harsh a way of putting it, since the idea is for both the novice and the master to decide whether the novice has a vocation, not whether the novice is tough enough to endure hardship.

We found out about Frank during one of the evening conferences. The purpose of these was to discuss problems relating to prayer and to consider subjects for the following day's meditations, all according to the suggestions and guidelines of the *Spiritual Exercises*. Since we were a small, tightly knit group, the absence of any individual was quickly noticed. As we waited in silence for Jim to appear, we probably thought that Frank was sick and had gone to the infirmary for a visit with Brother Bocabella. However, the first thing Jim said when he came in was that Frank had decided that the Jesuits were not for him and that he had departed during the day. Jim was very sensitive about the possible effect of this on the rest of us. He stressed the fact that this was no reflection on Frank's worth as a human being or as a Catholic. No stigma should be attached to anyone's decision to leave. These were welcome words to me, since now I entertained the first serious thoughts about leaving myself.

In reality, I had been thinking such thoughts even before I arrived at Bellarmine. But I was afraid that people would think less of me if I dropped out. I wasn't concerned about my parents, because I knew that they would accept whatever I did. They were always great about this. Aside from suggesting electrical engineering as a possible career for me, my dad (or my mom, either) never pushed any of us kids (I have a younger brother and sister) in any direction. To them, it wouldn't have mattered whether we were ditch diggers or corporation presidents. The Jesuits at McQuaid, however, were a different matter. Since I felt that their approval of me was in great part due to my performance, I feared their disapproval for leaving. But most of all it was Betsy's opinion that I was worried about. To maintain her approval I felt I would have to stay, but this would have deprived me of what I wanted. On the other hand, if I left to pursue her, she might think less of me and I would lose her anyway. And, of course, if I left, there was the troublesome issue of my sexuality, which I was still reluctant to face.

My thoughts were therefore conflicted and remained so until Frank's departure, which opened up a door for me. Suddenly, the thought of leaving no longer seemed so terrifying. I guess no one wanted to be the first to go. Within the next few days, I made up my mind. I would be the second person to leave. After me, several more would leave in fairly short order until things settled down around Christmas.

As expected, Jim Demske was great. He asked me some questions, basically just to see that I was okay. I think he wanted to make sure that the strain of the Long Retreat hadn't caused any emotional damage. He asked me what my plans were, and I told him that I wanted to go to college at some point. He said it might be possible to get into a college immediately, provided I contacted my guidance counselor as soon as I got home, which I did. And so, as I boarded the plane at the Plattsburgh airport, I said goodbye to my career as a Jesuit priest and anxiously pondered what was at best an uncertain future.

College

I left Bellarmine on a Tuesday, and by Friday I was on a bus headed for New York City. The guidance counselor at McQuaid had pulled some strings and arranged for me to attend Fordham College, a Jesuit institution in the Bronx. Due to the fact that I had missed the first four weeks of the fall semester, it would have been all but impossible for me to get into a school at this point. However, there were two huge points in my favor: my excellent academic record in high school and the fact that I had sacrificed my chance at college to become a Jesuit. And so I was offered three choices: Canisius College in Buffalo (where Jim Demske would eventually settle in as President), LeMoyne College in Syracuse, or Fordham. Once again, Betsy figured prominently in my decision. Although Canisius and LeMoyne were only an hour and a half away, and Fordham was over nine hours away (by bus), I chose Fordham because I thought it was the most prestigious. Also, Betsy's family was from the New York City area, and I thought that they would be impressed. The disadvantage, of course, was that I wouldn't be able to see Betsy as often; but this was outweighed by Fordham's higher academic and social standing. In the end, it made no difference. After a few clumsy attempts at courtship over the next several months, I finally gave up on Betsy. She would never be a factor in my life again.

There were many aspects to my college life; but since this chapter is mostly concerned with my spiritual formation, I will focus on that for now. It was in freshman year that I got my first taste of radical theology in the person of Augustine "Gus" Grady, S.J. Fortunately for me, I had been somewhat

26

prepared for him by the Jesuits at McQuaid and also at Bellarmine, who hinted that some of the "truths" in the *Baltimore Catechism* might be taken with a grain of salt. Aside from being exposed to the Form Critics, who argued that many if not all of the Biblical stories were not *literally* true, the biggest bombshell was the assertion that bread and wine were not really transformed into the body and blood of Christ during Mass. The bread and wine were merely symbolic. I remember that one of my fellow students nearly fell out of his chair when he heard this. His face turned red, and he was obviously shaken. I listened in shocked silence, trying to decide whether Gus was serious or whether he was just testing us.

The doctrine of Transubstantiation, the changing of the bread and wine into the body and blood of Christ, was one of the basic tenets of the Catholic Church. This was the central point of the Mass. In fact, one of the priests at McQuaid, who prided himself on being able to say a Mass in eight minutes, told us that if we were present at just this one moment during the Mass, we would have fulfilled our weekly obligation to attend Mass. St. Thomas Aquinas, the brilliant medieval theologian, had perfected an ingenious philosophical argument to explain what was essentially a mystery. It was called the Substance and Accidents theory, which asserted that every material object could be described in terms of its *accidents*, which were its physical properties, such as color, weight, shape, etc., and its *substance*, which was its essence (or Ideal, in Platonic terms). The key feature of this theory was that the substance of a thing could change while its accidents remained the same. Therefore, it was possible for bread and wine to look the same, smell the same, and taste the same but in essence to become the body and blood of Christ. Gus's approach was: why bother with such an outlandish theory? Why not just say that when the priest consecrates the bread and wine, Christ is spiritually present?

As a direct result of Gus's course, I began to look at religion differently. That is, when I looked at it at all.

For a while, I behaved as though I were still in the seminary. When the priest across the hall from us found out that I had been in the Jesuits, he asked me if I'd be interested in assisting him at daily Mass, which he said in his room. And so for the next several months, at 6:55 each morning, Fr. Wiley would poke his head in my room to make sure I was awake. I'd throw on some clothes, knock on his door, and we'd begin Mass promptly at 7:00 A.M. On the days when I didn't serve Mass for Fr. Wiley, I'd attend 7:30 Mass at the University Church. I guess at that point I didn't know which world, religious or secular, I was in.

Gradually, I became less concerned with religion. Other than my daily involvement with the Mass, I didn't think about it too much. I was still in love with Betsy. We had a couple of dates in November, but I was really looking forward to Christmas vacation. I knew that her high school would be having a holiday dance, and I was hoping that she would invite me. I suspected that she was still interested in her old boyfriend, who was now in his second year at Fairfield University. Both of us would be home for the holidays, so this would be an indication of which of us she preferred.

It wasn't me.

I had purposely avoided calling her, not wishing to appear too anxious. I was learning to play the game. Previously, when I had been confident in her feelings about me, I would not have hesitated to call her. It would not have occurred to me to hold back. But insecurity is the great destroyer of relationships. I waited for a call which never came. Instead, I received an invitation from another girl, one of Betsy's classmates. If I had had any sense, I would have realized that this girl never would have asked me unless she knew that Betsy was no longer interested in me, in which case I should have refused the invitation. Reluctantly, however, I accepted. There were probably two reasons: first, I wanted to see if Betsy would be there and if so with whom; second, if she were there, I wanted to show her that I didn't care whether she invited me or not. Game playing once again.

It turned out to be a big mistake. In the first place, I had a rotten time; and so did my date. Secondly, I did run into Betsy. She was with her former boyfriend; and, even though I tried to act nonchalant, I was deeply hurt. It was a devastating blow to my ego. Unbelievably, I repeated the same mistake five months later on an even bigger scale. Not only did I accept an invitation to Betsy's senior prom from another one of her friends. I even agreed to double date with Betsy and her beau—with me driving! The final humiliation came on the way home from the post-dance dinner, when I saw in the rearview mirror Betsy and her date making love in the back seat! I felt like a complete idiot at that point. Why had I set myself up for this?

Well, I had always been able to see a silver lining in the blackest of clouds, and this was it: my sense of anger and betrayal had finally overcome any residual feelings of love. From that point on, Betsy was no longer a factor in my life.

The Quest

The next thirty-odd years of my life can be summed up as the search for the ideal woman. I was seeking to recapture the magic of my first encounters with Betsy, only this time with a full dose of reality—meaning sex. Religion and morality receded farther and farther into the background as my obsession with sex intensified. The low point came in 1981, when I got a woman pregnant and then paid for an abortion (a "vaginal extraction," I believe they called it). I did, however, confess my actions to my parish priest, which showed that I still had some sense of guilt and shame. There were even periods when I attended Mass and took Communion, in spite of the fact that I was attempting to seduce every woman I met who was even remotely attractive. The incongruity of the situation didn't seem to bother me. Eventually, in the 90s, I stopped attending Mass altogether, except for weddings and funerals.

There were a few occasions, between bouts of womanizing, when I seriously thought about reapplying to the priesthood. The first was in late 1979 and/or early 1980. I had just quit one job and hadn't started my next. The reason for quitting was a vague dissatisfaction with my life. After several disappointing affairs, I thought that maybe I should move on to something else. For a few weeks, I considered going back to school to study astronomy, a field that had always fascinated me. But, after talking with an astronomy professor at the local university and also the curator of a planetarium, it became obvious that the field was already too crowded and that job prospects were bleak for the foreseeable future. It was then that I thought about the diocesan priesthood for the first time.

The diocesan or secular priesthood is different from the religious priesthood (e.g., the Jesuits) in several ways. First, priests who are members of a religious order take three vows: poverty, chastity, and obedience. Poverty simply means that the priest cannot own any property. It does not necessarily mean that the priest is poor. American Jesuits, especially the ones I stayed with in Los Angeles, live pretty well. Food and drink are abundant, as well as clothes, automobiles, computers, etc. However, these are all provided only for the priest's use and theoretically can be taken away at any time, depending on the needs of the Society. A diocesan priest, on the other hand, can retain any wealth that he has and is free to accumulate more. He is even paid a nominal salary by his diocese.

The vow of obedience means that a religious priest must do the will of his superiors. Normally, decisions are made by mutual agreement; but sometimes the priest has no choice. Diocesan priests, on the other hand, are under the jurisdiction of the local bishop. But a diocesan priest has a little more freedom of action. For example, the bishop would not normally interfere in financial or family matters. If the priest has a major disagreement with his bishop, he can resign and move somewhere else.

Over the years, the term *chastity* has been confused with *celibacy.* Catholic priests are required to be celibate, which simply means that they cannot get married. The vow of chastity, however, entails complete sexual abstinence. In practice, however, both terms amount to the same thing. It would be sinful for a diocesan priest to engage in sexual intercourse, just as it would be for a religious priest. The difference is that taking a vow of chastity would make the offense more serious. But such hairsplitting seems pointless.

Another major difference between diocesan and religious priests is their duties. Diocesan priests are usually assigned to parishes, whereas religious priests are normally engaged in teaching, both at the high school and university level. Parish work involves marriage and family counseling, saying Mass on weekends, presiding at weddings and funerals, visiting sick parishioners at home or in the hospital, and a host of other mundane matters. None of this appealed to me, especially the thought of having to deal with people's day-to-day problems. I was interested more in the academic world.

By the late fall of 1979, however, my attitude had begun to change. I was no longer a young man. I no longer had the sense of unlimited time, as I did when I was in high school. Since I had already been to college, I figured I could become a diocesan priest in four years. Becoming a Jesuit priest, however, could take considerably longer, especially if they wanted me to get an advanced degree. And so I arranged an interview with the head of the local diocesan seminary, just to check things out. We had an informal talk, but nothing was decided. Since it was the middle of the academic year, I wouldn't be able to enroll until the following September. There was plenty of time to ponder the matter, which I did.

Another idea I had at that time was writing, though I had no idea what to write about. I had never had an interest in or aptitude for writing fiction. While I liked poetry, I didn't think I could write it.

Which left nonfiction.

After years of writing term papers and more recently technical manuals, I figured I might be able to come up with some essays on various subjects, such as philosophy, religion, society, etc. By this time I had moved out of my parents' house into a small, shabby third-floor apartment (more like a room) in the bohemian section of town. I began to fancy myself an artist. However, after many weeks of restless reflection and wandering, I had produced only one sheet of single-spaced copy. My writing career wasn't looking too promising.

Out of boredom, I responded to an ad in the paper and took another full-time job at a large corporation. This time it was editing instead of writing. In two years, I quit that and was out on the street again. After a few short-lived jobs, including substitute teaching in the city schools, I was out of work for all of 1983. It was during this time that I made two trips: one to Boston and one to New York City, both in search of a lost vocation.

The Boston trip was in the early spring. The purpose of the trip was to attend a weekend of reflection at a Jesuit theological seminary in Weston, Massachusetts, just west of Boston. The agenda was designed to provide potential applicants to the Society of Jesus with a picture of what the Society was like and to provide ample opportunity to speak with the Jesuits themselves and the other attendees. There was also a Mass, a prayer service, and a group meeting where everyone could share his biography and thoughts about the future. When it was my turn, I tried to inject a note of levity into the proceedings by stating that my reason for being here was that I had been kicked out of the New York Province and that I was looking to the Boston Province for another chance.

This did get a few laughs, but I quickly settled down and gave a serious account of myself. Anyway, the highlight of the weekend for me was to be a private meeting with the Master of Novices in downtown Boston the next morning.

The new novitiate on Newbury Street was a complete departure from business as usual. The old novitiate, Shadowbrook, was in a remote section of the Berkshire Hills in western Massachusetts. In many ways it resembled Bellarmine College, my alma mater so to speak, which by this time had been closed down. The New York and Buffalo Provinces had been consolidated once again, and the novitiate was now located on the campus of LeMoyne College in Syracuse. At any rate, the Master of Novices, Joe McCormick, sat down with me in the parlor of this rather ordinary-looking house, whose occupants could have numbered no more than twenty, including staff and novices. Contrast this with Bellarmine College in 1963, where there were well over one hundred people. Times had definitely changed. We talked for an hour or so, but it was obvious to both of us that I wasn't ready to make a decision about re-entering the Jesuits. So I drove home, resolved only to do more "discernment," the process of trying to determine God's will.

Three months later, in July, I traveled by train to New York City to visit a former teacher from McQuaid. Again, the purpose of the trip was to assist in discernment. Despite the fact that I had made my intentions clear as to the reason for my visit, my former teacher assumed that there was an additional reason. From correspondence and personal contact with him in the years since graduation, I had learned that he was a homosexual and that he had been romantically interested in me from the very beginning of our acquaintance. This bothered me somewhat, but I wasn't too concerned because he had never made any advances. This time it was different. On the second evening of my visit, he indicated that he wanted me to spend the night with him in his room. I politely declined; and, after an uncomfortable night in my own room, left New York early the next morning. Before leaving the residence, I apologized for perhaps giving him the wrong impression; but he was obviously very unhappy with me. I was so upset that I went directly to the train station without inquiring about the departure schedule. A few days later, he sent me a nasty letter: What right did I have to pop in and out of his life at my whim and convenience, and take advantage of his affections? We've never had any further communication.

The train ride home proved to be very interesting. It was at least partial compensation for what otherwise had been a disastrous trip. By chance, I was seated next to a woman who wrote children's books. We chatted continuously for several hours before she left the train at Syracuse. I told her that I had had thoughts of becoming a writer myself. She gave me her name, address, and phone number and said that she would be glad to help me get started, even offering to help find a publisher if I ever got that far. Although I never tried to contact her, she did provide the encouragement I needed to continue a project I had begun a few months earlier: my autobiography.

Sometime around the end of January, 1983, I sat down at my electric typewriter and started to relate the story of my life. This came about as the result of a pamphlet I had read entitled *STUDIES in the Spirituality of Jesuits: Conversion as a*

Human Experience, by Paul V. Robb, S.J. The idea presented was simple: God speaks to us through the ordinary events of our lives. In other words, if we examine where we've been, we might get a pretty good idea of where we're headed—or should be headed. This was exactly what I needed. If I could analyze what had happened to me up to this point, I might be able to determine what God wanted me to do with my life. The best way to do this was to put everything down on paper and then look at it. Perhaps a pattern would emerge.

This had the added advantage of giving me something to write about. My previous attempt at writing had failed because I couldn't find an appropriate subject. Also, there was now a sense of urgency to complete the project. The sooner I could get the thing written, the sooner I would be able to discern God's will. I might even be able to get my autobiography published!

As usual, things didn't work out the way that I had planned. Although the writing proceeded well, at least in terms of volume (by the end of the year, I had produced over 500 single-spaced pages), it was unfocused. I put down everything I could think of in chronological order, occasionally stopping to analyze a significant event. Eventually, the project stalled, as I was distracted by another love affair and the necessity of finding employment. For a while, it appeared that the thrust of my life was toward the priesthood, but my continuing fascination with women put a halt to that.

Finally, in the late 80s and early 90s, my last serious attempt to reconsider the priesthood as a possible career consisted in attending theology courses at St. Bernard's Institute, the local diocesan seminary, which was now sharing the campus and resources of the Colgate Rochester Divinity

School. I ended up taking several courses as an unmatriculated student, hoping that at some point I would hear something in one of my classes which would push me to a decision. In the meantime, I would be accumulating credits, so that when the decision came, I would be in position to finish my training quickly. But I could not reach a decision. By the mid-90s, I stopped taking courses.

The Church

Over the centuries, the Catholic Church[8] has become what Judaism was at the time of Christ: a bureaucratic institution obsessed with maintaining discipline among its hierarchy and enforcing orthodoxy among its rank and file members. The New Testament is replete with examples of Christ's conflict with the Jewish authorities—a conflict that ultimately cost him his life. The essence of this conflict centered in the difference between the spirit and letter of the Jewish Law. Christ, himself a Jew, had been steeped in the Law, which was a complex system of doctrines and practices defining almost every aspect of Jewish life. Christ's mission was to reduce all of this, even the Ten Commandments, to two simple rules: love God and love your fellow men. This had the effect of undermining the authority of the Jewish leaders, who were the keepers and interpreters of the Law.

---

[8] I speak of the Catholic Church because it's the church I'm most familiar with. However, I suspect that much of what I say here could be applied to any other organized church.

Christ's followers no longer needed to worry about strict adherence to the Law. All they needed was the two simple rules. Understandably, the Jewish authorities felt threatened.

The same is true today. Bureaucracies, by nature, are more concerned with self-preservation than with serving their constituents. This is why they are cautious, slow-moving, and mendacious. If anything positive happens, it is usually the result of independent action on the part of the bureaucracy's members, who frequently must act in opposition to the official policy.

The Catholic Church is a prime example of this. Before and during World War II, the Catholic Church, as an institution, failed to denounce the racist, murderous, anti-religious policies of the Nazis, even though many individual Catholic leaders, such as Bishop Clemens von Galen, had protested within Germany itself. In our own time, the child abuse scandal illustrates how a bureaucracy instinctively reacts when it is attacked: it obfuscates, prevaricates, and, when all else fails, lies. This is not the kind of behavior one would expect from an institution which traditionally has been a bastion of morality.

I suppose the argument could be made that to throw open the Church archives for all to see would be to expose the Church to so many potentially damaging lawsuits as to bankrupt it. Well, so be it. Maybe the best thing to happen to the Church would be to wipe the slate clean and start all over again, thus restoring it to its original, pristine state. Unfortunately, success in the Church is measured by the number of priests and nuns, membership, weekly attendance, and, above all else, the amount of money in the collection basket. The Church has become a business. Much of the money collected is used simply to maintain itself. Many years ago, perhaps in the 50s during the time of Pope Pius XII, which coincided with the Eisenhower Administration, a time that we now look back upon as one of peace and stability, I heard someone say that the best thing that could happen to the Catholic Church was another persecution. Historically, the Church (meaning the individual members, as opposed to the institution) seems to flourish during times of great difficulty: the Roman persecutions, the barbarian invasions, the Nazi death camps, the Stalinist labor camps. Indeed, Alexander Solshenitsyn has provided moving testimony of Christ's presence in the Gulag.

As a Catholic myself, though not a practicing one in the traditional sense, I'm not too concerned about the future of the institutional Church. People have become accustomed to attending weekly Mass, regularly receiving the sacraments, and having easy access to priests and nuns. All of this is unnecessary. A once-in-a-lifetime exposure to the Mass and/or the Eucharist would be sufficient. Most of the people attending Christ's Sermon on the Mount undoubtedly never saw Him again, but their lives were transformed forever. When Christ departed, He promised to send the Holy Spirit, Who would be with us all days, even to the end of the world. What else do we need?

All that I have read or heard over the years has convinced me that the ultimate reality which we call God can only be approached indirectly. In the words of J.B.S. Haldane (*Possible Worlds,* 1927):

Now, my suspicion is that the universe is not only queerer than we suppose, but queerer than we *can* suppose . . . I suspect that there are more things in heaven and earth than are

dreamed of, in any philosophy [cf. Shakespeare, *Hamlet*].
That is the reason I have no philosophy myself, and must be
my excuse for dreaming.

In other words, we can only speak of God metaphori-
cally or symbolically. This is the reason Christ used parables
in his teaching. Religion itself becomes symbolic. And, as
with any symbol, it can be discarded when it no longer
works; i.e., provides insight and understanding. As I see it,
this is the meaning of the Incarnation: God became man in
the person of Jesus Christ because this was perhaps the best
way to give man some idea of what He was like.

In an interview given to William F. Buckley for *Firing
Line* in 1989, the renowned British journalist Malcolm
Muggeridge, who had sent shock waves throughout the liter-
ary world by converting to Catholicism late in life, was asked
whether he was apprehensive about the future of civilization
in light of all the problems in the world. Muggeridge responded by comparing the current world situation to that at
the time of Saint Augustine, when the Roman Empire was in
its final stages of dissolution just prior to the onset of the
Dark Ages. With barbarians literally at the gates, Augustine
was at work on his crowning achievement, *The City of God.*
In it, he contrasts the cities of Man, which are fleeting and
perishable, with the city of God, which is eternal and unassailable. Therefore, like Augustine, Muggeridge was not
concerned. All things, even evil, were part of God's plan and
would turn out all right in the end.

I don't know whether this is true or not, but it sounds
better than anything else I've come across.

Faith Kills

Nothing disturbs me more than the current situation in regard to international terrorism,[9] which I believe is as serious a threat to civilization as Fascism in the 30s and 40s or Russian/Chinese Communism during the Cold War. Particularly distressing is the fact that this abominable behavior is rooted in religion, which is commonly thought to exert a positive and healing influence in the world. But as I have tried to point out in this chapter and elsewhere, religion itself is at best an imperfect symbol of a reality which is essentially unfathomable. In other words, people are killing each other for reasons which are completely irrational. Not that war or killing is ever rational. But at least you could understand it if people were fighting for survival, as when the Russians resisted the Nazi invasion during the Second World War.

I think I understand, at least partially, the Muslims' hatred of western civilization, which they regard as a corrupting influence on their theocratic and theocentric society. Perhaps they feel that the West is actually controlling them through their oil. I, for one, would be perfectly happy to let the Muslim countries live in isolation, if that is their wish, even if it means a lessening of my ability to move around in my car. Unfortunately, oil is a critical commodity. The Arabs would probably not be willing to sacrifice their oil revenues for the sake of Islamic purity, nor would the West want them to. This

---

[9] As opposed to local or regional terrorism, such as the Protestant-Catholic conflict in Northern Ireland, which has not generally spilled over into the outside world.

41

leads, of course, to the inevitable interaction of cultures and religions, often resulting in misunderstanding and violence.

What I do find difficult to understand, though, is why a man on the street in Teheran should be so upset about a tribal conflict in Palestine. Why should he take it personally if the Jews and the Arabs cannot resolve their differences in a country that is hundreds of miles away? Does he believe that the Jews are bent on conquering the entire Middle East? Or in destroying Islam? An objective observer would have to concede that the Jews are the ones who are in danger of extinction. The Arabs would seem to be the ones with all the advantages: population, territory, economic power. And yet the entire Arab world is inflamed by what is in reality a neighborhood scrap. While I believe the majority of Jews and Arabs are eager to reach some kind of accommodation, if only for the simple and practical reason of survival, there are fanatics on both sides who are committed to sabotaging any kind of peace that does not annihilate the other side.

I must emphasize, however, that I'm not singling out Islam as the prime example of religious terrorism. In the first place, we're talking about a relatively small number of fanatics in a world population of hundreds of millions. I, for one, can't even say for sure whether the motivation is religious in nature. Perhaps the leaders of Al Qaida and other terrorist organizations are manipulating religious passions to acquire political power. Secondly, faith-based terrorism is not limited to Muslims. History, unfortunately, provides us with all too many examples of Christian, particularly Catholic, terror. One need only think of the current situation in Northern Ireland or the pogroms in Czarist Russia or the Spanish Inquisition.

How do you explain such incredibly idiotic behavior? A set of beliefs, passionately conceived, with little or no rational basis, cumulatively reinforced by centuries of conflict.

Pope John Paul II has implored the world never to allow religious differences to be the cause of violence. Unfortunately, his plea has not been heeded. Religion has been, and continues to be, a major source of conflict.

Today

As I stated in the Introduction, I believe there are five ways of apprehending the ultimate mystery of life:

- Mysticism (meditation or contemplative prayer)
- Epiphany
- Self-examination
- Observation and reflection
- Death

I've given up on mysticism because I don't trust my mind; that is, I don't think I can distinguish between a genuine communication with God and a figment of my imagination.

Epiphanies are unreliable. They can't be induced or anticipated.

Self-examination and observation/reflection are good methods to use while we're still alive; but, as we will see in the subsequent chapters, the results may not be definitive.

Death is probably the best bet; but I don't feel inclined to exercise that option just yet, unless it were as quick and clean as flipping a light switch. However, I don't think I'm afraid of it; nor will I take extraordinary measures to postpone it. After all, it could be the gateway to unimaginable joy, knowledge, and fulfillment. Or it may simply be the end of all we know, a sleep from which we never awake. Either way, it's okay with me. I don't think there are any other realistic possibilities. If death is something other than nothing, then I have a sneaking suspicion that it may resemble what Christianity has always said it was: resurrection and eternal life.

For the present, my attitude is: wait and see. For all my ruminations about life and death, I do not have a clear understanding of what human existence means. I don't know for certain why we're here, either collectively or individually. Over the years, I've developed a greater reverence for life, so much so that I'm distressed when any living creature dies.

I consider myself a religious person, in the sense that I'm a seeker of God, though I don't belong to any church. I have a soft spot for Catholicism, since I was raised a Catholic and spent most of my life within its orbit; but I don't observe any of its rites at present. The Jesuits taught me to regard the trappings of religion as symbolic of a more profound, mystical reality whose meaning can be approached only indirectly. It's unfortunate that men should be murdering each other in the name of God, but this is nothing new. The Roman persecutions, the Crusades, the Inquisition, the Holocaust, and now the Islamic Jihad are all testaments to man's inhumanity to man—and God.

Tomorrow

Despite the daily diet of bad news about people being killed around the world because of religious differences, I am an optimist. This is due to primarily to my Jesuit education—and my life experience.

As I look back on my own life, I realize that I have made many mistakes. For the first twenty years or so, I was prevented from making mistakes because my religious/moral indoctrination had been so strong that I was afraid even to attempt anything that might get me into trouble. The things that traditionally lead to problems, such as greed, ambition, and substance abuse, I wasn't interested in. The only area where I was vulnerable was sex, and even this was more a matter of curiosity than passion.

Ever since the age of reason, around seven, I had been fascinated by women. It began with the mass introduction of television in the early 1950s, when for lack of much original programming, NBC (which was for several years the only network available in our area) showed hundreds of movies and comedy shorts, some of which haven't been seen again, even on the cable and satellite channels. I was particularly attracted to the B-Westerns of the 1930s, where the heroes were courageous and upright, the villains were thoroughly evil, and the heroines were quintessentially feminine and remotely beautiful. Sex was completely absent from these movies. The hero might kiss the heroine in the closing scene, but often the kiss would be obscured by a fadeout or the hero's horse stepping in front of the camera or someone interposing a hat. Often, the hero wouldn't kiss the heroine at all. Interestingly, this lack of explicit physical affection made the whole thing terribly romantic, almost idyllic. And this is where I got my idea of what male-female relations should be.

A few years later, I started noticing women's clothes, particularly the dresses, stockings, and high heels. This intensified my superficial attraction to women to such a degree that, by the time I had my first real date with a fully decked out woman, I was completely overwhelmed. But it wasn't sexual desire. It was the thrill of being close to such a magnificent creature, of possessing her in a way, even if it was only for a brief moment. From that point on, the priesthood became a distant second on my list of priorities.

As I've said before, this was the pivotal event of my life. So much so, that I've thought it was divinely induced. Almost from the moment of Betsy's phone call, I considered the possibility that God may have arranged it. But this didn't make sense. On the surface, it would seem that God was working against Himself by effectively preventing me from entering the priesthood. After all, there was no way I could keep my mind on a religious vocation after meeting Betsy. But as those of us who have believed at one time or another know, God works in mysterious ways, ways that are contradictory to our way of thinking.

This opens up a whole field of speculation. If there is a God, a Supreme Being, to what extent does He control things? Is there such a thing as free will? Can we choose to separate ourselves from Him? I don't know the answers to these questions or a hundred other related ones; and at this stage of my life, I don't care. As far as I know, I've always acted in freedom. *Perhaps the sum total of all my decisions has resulted in a predetermined condition.*

In the beautiful closing scene of *Brideshead Revisited*, Charles Ryder, the hero and narrator of the story, realizes this when he enters the chapel at the Brideshead estate, which has been requisitioned by the British military during World War II. Despite his previous close association with the former owners of the estate, the Catholic Marchmains, Charles has remained an atheist. All of the family members have gone off to their separate destinies, including the two rebels, Sebastian and Julia. Sebastian, Charles' closest friend since their days at Oxford, ends up as a drunken hanger-on at a monastery in North Africa. Julia, with whom Charles had had an adulterous affair, rejected Charles to pursue a life of service. Ironically, both Sebastian and Julia had spent most of their lives trying to distance themselves from the influence of their pious mother, only to find that they can't escape from God. Charles, who had been devastated by Julia's rejection, especially since it had been prompted by Julia's rediscovery of her faith, a faith that had always been incomprehensible to him, finally begins to understand:

The chapel showed no ill effects of its long neglect; the art-nouveau paint was as fresh and as bright as ever; the art-nouveau lamp burned once more before the altar. I said a prayer, an ancient, newly learned form of words, and left, turning towards the camp; and as I walked back, and the cook-house bugle sounded ahead of me, I thought:

The builders did not know the uses to which their work would descend; they made a new house with the stones of the old castle; year by year, generation after generation, they enriched and extended it; year by year the great harvest of timber in the park grew to ripeness; until, in sudden frost, came the age of Hooper [Charles' young adjutant]; the place was desolate and the work all brought to nothing; *Quomodo sedet sola civitas*. Vanity of vanities, all is vanity.

And yet, I thought, stepping out more briskly toward the

camp, . . . that is not the last word; it is not even an apt word; it is a dead word from ten years back.

Something quite remote from anything the builders intended has come out of their work, and out of the fierce little human tragedy in which I played; something none of us thought about at the time: a small red flame—a beaten copper lamp of deplorable design, relit before the beaten-copper doors of a tabernacle; the flame which the old knights saw from their tombs, which they saw put out; that flame burns again for other soldiers, far from home, farther, in heart, than Acre or Jerusalem. It could not have been lit but for the builders and the tragedians, and there I found it this morning, burning anew among the old stones.[10]

We go through life in search of happiness. We try all manner of things: wealth, romance, power, excitement. In the end, if we haven't become hopelessly entangled in the pursuit, we may come to the conclusion that all our exertions don't amount to a hill of beans. In my own case, I have decided that I am incapable of making myself happy through any effort of my own. I have reached a state of detachment, where I am willing to accept whatever happens. This is not the same as indifference, however. I am not insensitive to what happens in the world around me. I do what I can[11] to make things better, but I'm content to let God handle the big picture.

---

[10] Evelyn Waugh, Brideshead Revisisted (Back Bay Books, New York, 1999), pp. 350–351.

[11] Apropos of this attitude, one of my favorite sayings is the motto of the Christophers: "It is better to light one candle than to curse the darkness."

3. Epiphanies

Larry: You were right. Something very strange *did* happen to me.

Holy Man: I know . . . Tell me.

Larry: It was just at that moment before night ends and day begins, when the whole world seems to tremble in the balance. Gradually the light began to filter through the darkness, like some mysterious figure stealing through the trees. And then the first rays of the sun came up. The mountains, the mist caught in the trees—I'd never before felt or seen anything like it.

Holy Man: I know . . . I come here often.

Larry: I felt that I'd been released from my body, that I was suspended in mid-air and that all the things that had been confused before suddenly became clear to me. I had a sense of knowledge more than human. I felt that I'd broken away and was free. I felt that if it lasted another minute, I . . . I'd die. And yet I was willing to die if I could just hold onto it because—for that one moment I had the feeling that—

Holy Man: You and God were one.

Larry: Yes.

—The Razor's Edge

Background

The school year 1964–1965, when I was a sophomore at Fordham College in the Bronx, was particularly traumatic. On a microcosmic scale, it was akin to what Western Civilization must have felt during and after the First World War: confusion and disillusionment.

As I have related in the previous chapter, by the time I finished high school, I had forced myself to become a disciplined and dedicated, if not inspired, student. This was due primarily to a supreme act of will on my part, sparked by a charismatic teacher. The study habits that I had mastered in high school carried me through my first year of college where, despite missing the first five weeks of class due to a brief sojourn in the Society of Jesus, I had posted a near-perfect grade-point average. My prospects for a brilliant academic future seemed bright indeed.

However, the seeds of my eventual downfall were planted in that first year of college. It all began with my friendship with Henry Bender. Like most of my significant human relationships, this one started as a result of the other person taking the initiative. Since Henry and I were both Classics Majors, we ended up in the same Latin and Greek classes, which probably explains how we ended up in the same English class as well (because of the necessity of avoiding scheduling conflicts with courses outside our major). At any rate, Henry, who was much more outgoing than I was, began talking to me almost as soon as I enrolled. Maybe he was intrigued by the fact that I started so late, as well as by the fact that I was an ex-Jesuit. Before long, we became inseparable. Not only did we see each other at least two hours every day in class, but we also lived in the same dorm, albeit in different wings. We used to hang around together on weekends, too, when we would toss a football between bouts of studying or simply lounge about in his room, which his roommate vacated every Saturday and Sunday, since his home was in nearby Westchester County.

By the time of the Kennedy Assassination in November of 1963, we had become best friends. I vividly remember how bummed out we were the weekend after that horrible event, when we just lay on the beds in Henry's room, listening to music on his reel-to-reel tape recorder, unable to study or play.

It was sometime during the winter that we decided to become roommates for the following year. Although fraternities were not allowed at our school, there was a process by which the students could determine who would be admitted to their dormitory. Whereas the incoming freshmen had no choice as to their room assignments in the freshman dormitories, the upperclassmen had considerable discretion in selecting their living quarters, including the option of not living on campus. The upper class dormitories consisted of seven buildings (actually one building with seven sections), lettered A through G. Over the years, each of these buildings had developed a distinctive style and reputation. For example, A-House was regarded as the academic building, where the students were expected to maintain a high grade-point average above all else. B-House was considered to be the best all-around dorm, where academic excellence was highly regarded, but so was a healthy interest in sports or entertainment, which could include the theater, the opera, or simply going out to a good restaurant now and then. C, D, and E were

51

sort of middle of the road, with no particular distinction of any kind. F and G were considered to be the "animal houses," which were occupied by jocks, party people, hoods, and various other academic non-performers—including people who had nowhere else to go.

Students in all seven houses were permitted to hold auditions for the purpose of selecting which freshmen would fill the upcoming vacancies. I guess this would be loosely analogous to the process of pledging for a fraternity, with two important differences: (1) no trial, tribulation, or torture was allowed beyond the auditioning interview and (2) every student was guaranteed a room somewhere. A student could request to be placed in a specific house without submitting to the interview process, but students chosen by the interviewing committee would be given priority. To my recollection, not all the houses conducted selection interviews. But A and B certainly did.

Henry and I decided to try for B. (Students had the option of applying individually or as roommates.)

The only problem was that I was opposed to the idea of having to submit to an interview. Somehow, it offended my dignity. Also, during the previous four years, I had become something of a prig. I took myself much too seriously and would have found it difficult to endure the questions and antics of the interviewers, even though much of it was transparently mischievous and intended to be taken in the spirit of harmless fun. Henry instinctively knew this. For example, in response to a question which I found offensive, Henry took it (rightly) as a joke and turned it back on his interrogator, which produced smiles all around, except from me. As I became increasingly uncomfortable and resentful, Henry warmed to his task and seemed to be enjoying himself, as did the interrogators.

In the end, Henry wound up in B-House and I didn't. I'm not sure whether it was because I was rejected or because we decided not to become roommates. I think by the end of freshman year some strains had developed in our friendship. I was beginning to feel resentful of Henry in some ways, though I don't think he felt that way about me. I was probably the one who decided that we shouldn't become roommates, but I don't remember precisely why. However, at the end of freshman year, we still considered ourselves to be close friends.

The fact that I didn't get a room in B-House, with or without Henry, had profound consequences for me. I thought about asking my current roommate, Chuck Merz, if he wanted to room together again; but he had already asked another guy, Hank Wasilausky, a fellow chemistry major. After a slow start, Chuck and I had become pretty good friends. More importantly, we had become very comfortable with each other. This might have been due to the fact that because we were majoring in such diverse fields (classical languages versus chemistry), there was no competition between us. I ended up becoming pretty friendly with Hank, too. And it was through my acquaintance with both Chuck and Hank that I met Carlos Quirce, who was to become one of my all-time great friends. But I digress.

As the result of a non-decision, I completed freshman year not knowing or caring where I would be living the following year.

Sometime during the summer, I received notification that I had been assigned to G-House. Normally, I would have been placed in either a six- or eight-man suite. Each house consisted of four floors with a central stairway. The six-man suites were on one side of the stairway (the left, I believe, as you got off the stairway), and the eight-man suites were on the right. The reason for this asymmetrical design was that on the side of the six-man suites was a separate suite consisting of two rooms and bath. This suite had its own entrance door. As you entered, the bath was on the left. One room was straight ahead, and the other was to the right. These two-room suites were intended for the floor monitors, who were either Jesuit faculty or graduate students (one monitor per suite). As a reward for putting up with the undergraduates, the lay graduate students were not required to pay for their rooms. (I'm not sure what reward the Jesuit monitors got—canonization, perhaps?)

For some reason, the two-room suite on the fourth floor was not assigned to a monitor. Instead, it was occupied by two seniors: John Kelly on the left and Pat O'Connor on the right. Pat's room had an extra bed and desk, which is where I ended up.

John, a psychology major, and Pat, a math major, were two of the biggest (pardon the vulgarity) fuck-offs that ever came down the pike. John, who attended most of his classes, hardly ever cracked a book—a psychology book, that is. During the week, in the evenings, he would listen to the radio, read magazines, talk to his girlfriend, sometimes meet her on our campus, sometimes on hers (i.e., Marymount College, an exclusive women's college in upper Westchester County), or even sometimes at her parents' apartment, which was in a high-rise off Fordham Road, within easy walking distance of our campus.

Regina, John's girlfriend, was wonderful: not beautiful, not sexy, but extremely attractive in a number of subtle ways. Whenever I was fortunate enough to see her (which was only half a dozen times all year, including a double date with her sister which John arranged), she was tastefully dressed (in those days, college women, as well as college men, dressed in business attire). Her manners were impeccable, but there was nothing forced or phony about her. Of course, I fell in love with her immediately. If she hadn't been John's girl, I would have pursued her. Unfortunately for me, John and Regina were serious; though not officially engaged, they intended to get married soon after graduation.

Pat, on the other hand, was in many ways the complete opposite of John. Like me, he was socially inept. Also like me, he was deficient in the fashion department. The two of us barely satisfied the requirements of the dress code (dress shirt, jacket, and tie). John, on the other hand, sent his shirts out to be professionally laundered, along with his considerable collection of suits, slacks, and sport jackets. Pat and I were lucky if we could come up with a clean shirt every day—that is, on the days we went to class.

Academically, the year 1964–1965 began where the previous year had left off. My study habits were still solid, I attended all my classes, and I had good relationships with all my professors, particularly Herb Musurillo, who had taught me Greek tragedy (the *Medea* of Euripides) the year before. Actually, Herb wasn't one of my professors for the fall semester; but we had become such good friends the year before that we continued to socialize on a regular basis. The Classics Department was so small that everybody knew each other. Herb encouraged Henry and me to stop in to see him as often as we could, which was just about every day. Through Herb, we became good friends with one of his colleagues, Peter Pouncey, a new professor who had just come over from England, where he had been a Jesuit scholastic. I'm not sure how far along Peter had been in his Jesuit training; but it was evident that he had completed most of the course work for his Ph.D. in Classics (at Oxford University, I believe). Henry and I were enrolled in Peter's History of Greece course. Before long, the four of us (Henry, Peter, Herb, and I) formed our own informal social club. In addition to seeing each other in class and in the Classics Department offices, we frequently met for pizza, beer, and perhaps a movie on weekends. Most often, our mode of transportation was Pete's Volkswagen bug.

During the late fall of 1964 things began to change. It all started with my roommate's sleeping habits. Between classes, I used to stop back at the room to drop off my books. Depending on the length of the break and the time of day, I would either go out to the deli for something to eat, throw the football around with Henry and/or Pete, or read/study. Increasingly, I would find Pat sleeping in his bed when I entered the room. I didn't pay too much attention at first, but eventually Pat's constant presence in bed began to affect my study habits. Not wishing to disturb him, I would gather up my books and head for the library. One afternoon, as I was preparing to go out, Pat woke up. I apologized for disturbing him. Then we started to talk. Up to that point, we had not had an extended conversation. Our relationship had been cordial, but superficial. But now we began to learn some things about each other.

Pat was from Brooklyn, which was about one to two

hours away, depending on which subway train you had to take. Despite this relative closeness, Pat almost never went home. In fact, it seemed that he hardly ever communicated with his family. This was in marked contrast to John (also from Brooklyn), who was gone almost every weekend and often on weeknights as well. I suppose this is one of the reasons why Pat and I became such close friends: we were alone together much of the time in a room that was isolated from the rest of the dorm. Also, we were both intellectual, introspective types who were more comfortable in solitude than in the superficial conviviality of a college dormitory. And we were terrified and fascinated by women.

Pat's constant presence in bed had a simple explanation: he was cutting classes by day and studying (mostly linguistics) by night. At the start of the school year, he did attend all his classes; but it didn't take him long to decide which ones he was interested in and which ones he wasn't. Or, more precisely, which ones he could safely cut and which ones he couldn't. It turned out that he could cut all of them. Three of his six courses were in math. Pat was an accomplished mathematician; also, the Mathematics Department, like the Classics Department, was very small. Professors who knew you (and after a couple of years they all did) would give you a lot of slack, provided you had demonstrated ability and/or interest. Pat apparently had. His philosophy and theology courses were required for all seniors. Professors in these courses were not likely to give the seniors a hard time, as long as they passed the exams (which could be crammed for). That left Pat's only elective course, linguistics. Ironically, this was the only course that Pat had any enthusiasm for and the one which primarily occupied his nocturnal studies. He was particularly fascinated by certain sounds, sounds which apparently existed in other languages but not English. Two of these were to play a significant role in our relationship.

In retrospect, my friendship with Pat was one of my closest—and certainly the strangest. By the spring semester, we were communicating by sounds and gestures—the words, if any, would come later. We got to be so comfortable with each other that we felt free to say anything at any time, from the sublime to the ridiculous. We could start a conversation by quoting Aristotle—or Bugs Bunny. We talked for hours on end.

Which is what led to my downfall, as a student.

Instead of studying on the breaks between classes or after class, I found myself talking to Pat. If he was sleeping, I might get into my bed, too. Also, I was beginning to lose interest in my studies. Part of this could be explained by my professors, who as a group were not as stimulating as those in my freshman year. Part of it was due to the fact that my two roommates were seniors, whose attitude was understandably different from mine. And I began to have doubts as to the worth of what I was doing. The study and teaching of the Classics seemed to be a particularly useless profession. One generation of students would learn the Classics, only to pass it on to the next, with little impact outside this rather exclusive club. I asked myself whether I really cared about my studies or whether I was just interested in getting high marks as a way of validating my existence. To be perfectly honest, I felt that I had nothing else going for me other than a great report card. But even that was about to change.

Despite my struggles, I was able to finish the first semester with a very high average, only a few percentage points below the high water mark of the spring semester of freshman year. But it was obvious that I had limped to the finish line. Only my momentum had got me there.

As the spring semester got underway, I began to cut classes. Not all classes, not all the time; but enough that people started noticing and being concerned. Foremost, of course, were Henry, Herb, and Pete. I was enrolled in another one of Herb's courses, Introduction to Patristic Literature, which dealt with the early Church Fathers, such as Origen, Tertullian, and Jerome. Also, I was enrolled with Pete again, this time in a history of the Roman Empire. My English, Latin, and Philosophy professors were the same. My Honors Program seminar on Evolution was replaced by one on Drama. This met once a week for two hours. There were only a dozen students in this course, so I thought it best not to cut it, since my absence would be conspicuous. Also, this course was a requirement for the Honors Program, which at this point I hadn't decided to abandon.[1] Meanwhile, the strains in my relationship with Henry were becoming more pronounced, despite the fact that I visited his home outside Philadelphia on a couple of weekends in late winter and early spring.

By the time of my second visit to Henry's house, things really began to unravel. My academic life was a shambles, I wasn't getting along well with Henry, and I had just had an emotionally draining experience with Henry's younger sister, who had had the great misfortune of becoming infatuated

---

[1] The big advantage of being in the Honors Program was the opportunity to spend junior year abroad.

with me. I say misfortune, because at that time I could not possibly have had any kind of normal relationship with a woman, even though I was convinced it was the only thing in life worth having. In practical terms, this meant that I would reject any woman who showed any interest in me. Which is exactly what happened with Henry's sister, causing a further deterioration of my friendship with Henry.

All of this is by way of background for my first epiphany, which I will now relate.

Epiphany No. 1

It was a Sunday morning in late April. I was attending Mass at the Fordham University Church with my high school friend John Amann (in addition to John and myself, there were two other former McQuaid classmates at Fordham, neither of whom I saw more than half a dozen times there). When I entered the church that morning, I was particularly depressed. Final exams were coming soon, and I was beginning to wonder whether there was any point in taking them. I had cut a significant number of my classes; I had done hardly any studying; and several research papers were coming due, none of which I had even started.

Suddenly, about halfway through the Mass, an intense feeling of calm began to come over me, as though I were in a bathtub and the warming waters were slowly rising, gradually covering my body. Even my friend John, who was standing next to me, noticed something was happening. He gave me a nudge, accompanied by a quizzical look, to which I responded with a smile. The feeling persisted for several minutes. By the end of the Mass, I was convinced that everything would be all right, no matter what I did. John and I didn't say anything as we walked away from the church, and I don't think I ever told anyone about my experience.

A day or so later, I decided to leave school.

This was a direct result of my epiphany in the church which, if nothing else, had given me a feeling of invincibility. I was going to cast my fate to the wind and let the future unfold before me. As it turned out, it didn't take long for fate to intervene.

I had only been home for a couple of days when I received a phone call from New York. John Kelly was on the line, accompanied by Pat. Somehow, they had gotten my home phone number from school officials, probably through the registrar's office, which must have taken considerable doing, since obtaining personal information from a bureaucratic institution is always difficult. I had notified John and/or Pat of my departure (I think I had told them the night before I left or possibly the following morning). Beyond the perfunctory weak protest, they didn't say much when I left. However, after discussing the matter off and on for the next day or so, they decided that they had been at least partially responsible for my academic collapse. This is what had led them to contact me.

They pleaded with me to come back. They tried to encourage me by saying that there was still plenty of time left to get myself straightened out, provided I acted quickly. As I listened (John did most of the talking, with Pat chiming in a word or two of agreement), I realized that I would indeed return. In fact, I boarded a bus the very next morning. During the tedious eight-hour ride, I reflected that it wasn't John or Pat's arguments that had persuaded me to go back. It was simply the fact that they had called. They had cared enough to make the effort. I think that most people, then and now, would have shrugged their shoulders and dismissed the whole affair by saying it was none of their business. They would have immersed themselves back into their own problems and pleasures without giving me another thought. And I wouldn't have blamed them. I probably would have done the same thing myself, had I been in John or Pat's position. I certainly wasn't expecting them to call—it came as a complete surprise.

I will always be grateful to both of them.

Not that this was the turning point in a life of great significance or accomplishment. I went on to finish college all right, after a few bumps here and there; but I haven't done anything particularly meaningful or momentous with my life—at least not yet. I'm still very much on the road and searching. If John and Pat hadn't called, there's a high probability that I wouldn't have returned to school. This, in turn, would have meant being drafted into the army eventually or perhaps enlistment in one of the other armed forces. God knows what the consequences of that would have been. At that time, the prospect of service in Vietnam was scary, but not morally abhorrent. The military was not in disrepute yet. That would take another year or two, as the casualties mounted and the shortcomings of the South Vietnamese regime became more apparent. After graduation from college and a brief stint as a high school English teacher, I did end up enlisting in the U.S. Coast Guard, despite misgivings that I was compromising my opposition to the war.

Epiphany No. 2

My second epiphany occurred in January of 2002. In the intervening thirty-seven years, as one might expect, profound changes had occurred in my life. At the most basic level, geography, I was now living with my wife at a remote cabin in the forested hills of upstate New York, as opposed to the frenzied streets of New York City. I had exchanged the altruistic idealism of my youth for the pragmatic business of survival. Instead of English literature, I was now teaching the repair and maintenance of medical laser printers—that is, when such employment was available, which increasingly it wasn't.

In January of 2002, my financial/employment position was actually pretty good. Although my teaching opportunities were dwindling, some other prospects had materialized, such as the development of a new training program and the revision of two old ones.

My second epiphany, as my first, occurred during Mass at a Catholic church. This time it was a funeral Mass for my Aunt Bernadine, who had died at the ripe old age of ninety-five. Aunt Bern, as she was called, represented the happiest times of my youth, which coincided with the decade of the 1950s. Her seven children—my first cousins—were all older than I. She herself had come from a large family (ten, nine of whom survived childhood). She was the second oldest, but the first to get married. Hence, her oldest son Edward (named after her husband) was almost as old as my father, who was the second youngest of Aunt Bern's siblings. As I was growing up, around the age of seven or eight, all of Aunt Bern's kids were either married or soon to be. To them, *I* must have seemed a pesky little nuisance. To me, though, *they* seemed glamorous and exciting. They were driving cars and doing lots of other things that I hoped to be doing someday. At the family get-togethers, they would bring their girl friends or boy friends or spouses. I so much wanted to be part of their world; but, naturally, they paid little attention to me or my efforts to amuse them. If I were lucky, they might tease me or toss me in the lake. Sometimes, when we were all in the water, I would sneak up behind them and grab them around the legs or neck. They would good-naturedly throw me off, and that would be the end of it. But I would usually try again later.

On that gray, sleety January morning, as the Mass began, my thoughts were wandering. I had stopped going to Mass regularly a long time ago. The liturgical aspect of the Mass had never interested me, even during my most devout period. I looked around the church to see who was there. Most of Aunt Bern's brothers and sisters were dead. Of the three still alive, one was in Florida and too old to travel; the two in Rochester were in no condition to attend, though all three were still mentally competent. Some of my cousins were also dead: Aunt Bern's two oldest children, Edward and Eileen, had passed away a few years earlier, as well as two of her nephews who were only in their fifties when they died.

Late in the service, after Holy Communion had been distributed, my cousin Jack stepped to the right lectern, where the first two scripture passages had been read earlier. Jack, who was Aunt Bern's second oldest son, was everybody's favorite cousin. Not only was he very good-looking; he was perhaps the one of Aunt Bern's children who most closely resembled her in temperament, which is to say he was the most appealing. There was something about him which attracted you, whether he was doing the polka with his wife Mary Ann or playing the drums or just talking. So it was logical that he would be the one to say some things about Aunt Bern as a kind of eulogy or final sendoff.

He started to relate an incident that occurred at the dinner table when they were all kids. It must have been in the early 1940s, after the younger children had all been born but before the older ones had left home. The incident, which was probably a faux pas, such as a breach of etiquette or a clumsy accident, was intended to illustrate Aunt Bern's gentleness, patience, and humor, which were her most salient qualities. As Jack filled in the details, he began to get tearful. Simultaneously, I was overcome by a powerful desire to have been present, not as a participant, which would of course violate the laws of causality, but merely as an observer. For although this particular incident occurred before I was born, it reminded me of other, similar, incidents which I had either observed or participated in. Jack broke down completely as he finished his story. I think he had wanted to tell some additional stories, but he was obviously unable to continue. Meanwhile, as Jack stepped down, I continued to be enthralled by the idea of visiting the past.

Then it hit me: the moment of insight which signifies an epiphany. For years, I had been troubled by what I considered to be a contradiction at the center of Christianity: Why did God create the cosmos, only to have his Son, Jesus Christ, renounce it in the Gospels? The traditional answer, which had never really satisfied me, was that God had created the world of time and space as a preparation for eternity; i.e., the Kingdom of God. The world was not an end in itself, but the

65

means to an end. This leads naturally to another question: If the world is not an end in itself, what should we be doing here? Is anything here worth doing? Why not trot off to a monastery and prayerfully wait for the end, as many in ancient and medieval times did?

Then I started thinking about the difference between time and eternity. Sometime long ago I had heard that the difference was simply this: in time, events occur sequentially; in eternity, events occur simultaneously. Immediately, I was struck by a technological analogy: the difference between a videotape and a CD (or DVD). On a tape, to get to Scene 4, you have to pass through Scenes 1, 2, and 3 first. On a CD or DVD, you can jump directly to any scene you want, which means in essence that you have instant access to any event.

Then the final connection: Maybe our purpose here is to participate in the making of a gigantic DVD, which will consist of billions of individual tracks, each representing the entire life of one human being, with all the events captured in sequence. In other words, at the end of time, we will have compiled a complete video library of every human life that has occupied this planet (and perhaps other planets as well). This will be available in DVD format, where it will be possible to skip to any point in time and view the events for any length of time.

So maybe I can experience the dinner table incident after all!

The idea of each person making his/her own home movie, so to speak, relates to a concept in recent theological discussions called *co-creation,* in which man does not merely respond to God's creative power passively but actually participates in it; i.e., man and God are partners in shaping the world. It also ties in with an idea proposed by the physicist Frank Tipler who, in his book *The Physics of Immortality,* asserts that

> . . . theology is nothing but physical cosmology based on the assumption that life as a whole is immortal. A consequence of this assumption is the resurrection of everyone who has ever lived to eternal life. Physics has now absorbed theology; the divorce between science and religion, between reason and emotion, is over.[2]

The physical basis of his theory is cybernetics: each human being who ever lived will achieve immortality by being stored as a computer simulation in memory.

I have no idea whether any of this is true. All I know is that my experience at the funeral Mass was overwhelming. Perhaps it will prove to be transforming as well. I guess I'll have to die to find out (when my videotape, DVD, or data file is complete).

---

[2] Frank J. Tipler, *The Physics of Immortality: Modern Cosmology, God and the Resurrection of the Dead* (New York, Doubleday, 1994), p. 338.

4. Love

Paul: Holly, I'm in love with you.
Holly: So what?
Paul: So what? So plenty. I love you. You belong to me.
Holly: No. People don't belong to people.
Paul: Of course they do.
Holly: I'm not gonna let anyone put me in a cage.
Paul: I don't want to put you in a cage. I want to love you.
Holly: It's the same thing.
Paul: No, it's not.

—Breakfast at Tiffany's

Overview

Nothing in this life causes human beings as much misery (or as much exhilaration, for that matter) as romantic love. I found this out when I was seventeen, in the midst of my first love affair. Until that time, being unhappy consisted in missing an opportunity to go swimming or in striking out in the bottom of the ninth inning with the winning run on base.

I had no intention of falling in love when I began my senior year of high school in September, 1962. The idea of becoming a Jesuit priest had been percolating in my mind for some time, and it was just starting to take its final form. I had

68

fantasized about women, of course. I was particularly entranced by the way they looked when they were all dressed up. There were a couple of girls on the bus that I was attracted to, and I had even thought about asking them out; that is, if I could ever get up enough courage to talk to them, which I didn't. Actually, I was simultaneously fascinated and terrified by women. To my relief, the priesthood presented itself as a way out of this dilemma.

My brief love affair[1] with Betsy illustrates the serendipitous nature of reality. This was a girl I did not know, who all of a sudden, out of the blue, called me up and asked me to a school dance. My initial reaction was to decline the invitation, figuring what was the point; but then it occurred to me that it might be a good idea to acquire some social experience before they locked me up in a seminary for ten years.

The morning after the dance, I was in love.

I had begun making inquiries about the process of admission to the Jesuits almost as soon as I returned to school from summer vacation. The guidance counselor wisely told me to make sure that I applied to some colleges also, just in case I were to change my mind about the Jesuits. At the time of Betsy's call, I had pretty much decided to enter the Jesuits, though my decision had not been revealed to anyone except my best friend Phil who, unbeknownst to me, was also considering the Jesuits. But as of October 19, the date of the dance, all options were still open to me.

It must have been a week or so later when my section of the senior class went on retreat at LeMoyne College in Syra-

---

[1] If you can call it that—I never kissed her, even in friendship.

cuse. For those of you not familiar with the Catholic faith, a retreat is period of prayer and reflection, lasting anywhere from one to thirty days, usually in a quiet, secluded place. The retreat, under the supervision of a retreat master, offers opportunities for both individual and group reflection. Each participant also has the opportunity to meet privately with the retreat master. The reason LeMoyne was chosen was that, in addition to providing a suitable retreat setting for a fairly large number of students, it gave the students a taste of college life. The retreat master, a middle-aged Jesuit priest named Father Kelly, was presumably on the faculty and could therefore answer questions about various aspects of the college.

When it was my turn to meet with Father Kelly, I immediately told him of my intention to enter the Jesuits. But I also mentioned my recent date with Betsy and asked him for advice on whether I should continue seeing her. However, I wasn't completely honest with him. I didn't describe the intensity of my feelings about Betsy. He probably got the impression that I was pretty comfortable with my decision to enter the Jesuits. He therefore advised me that it would serve no purpose to pursue a relationship with Betsy.

Within a week or so of my return from the retreat, I met Betsy and told her of my decision to apply for admission to the Society of Jesus. In my heart, though, I was not sure that this was what I wanted to do. I was in love, and nothing could change that. For the next year, I would be on a rollercoaster ride of emotions, alternating between elation and despair, unable to control my feelings. Looking back, I'm surprised that I was able to function at all.

Attempting to Duplicate the Past

My love affair with Betsy ultimately failed. It had been a fantasy, at best, but it had also been the most intense experience of my life. For the next thirty plus years, I sought to recapture its magic, this time entirely through my own effort. Having tasted the joy of romantic love, I was determined not to wait for fate to intervene. I took my first tentative steps at an afternoon social in the middle of my freshman year of college, when I struck up a conversation with one of the neighborhood girls in the Bronx. The following year, my uncle in New Jersey fixed me up with the daughter of one of his neighborhood friends. She was home from college for the weekend, and I went out to my uncle's place from New York. I wasn't particularly attracted to her physically; but she had an enthusiastic, outgoing personality and became the recipient of my first good-night kiss.

As the years wore on, I pursued many women. Invariably I was attracted by their physical appearance or by the way they dressed or both. Most of these relationships didn't last beyond one or two dates (that is, if I could get a date—many times I pursued a woman without ever getting to first base, as it were). On one or two occasions, I fell head over heels in love—but these affairs were totally one-sided on my part.

I began to despair of ever finding someone to love. Despite all my efforts, all my tricks, all my subterfuges—and there were some ingenious ones—I had come up empty. The best you could say was that I had acquired experience. I had learned to relax more with women, enjoy their company, even accept their affection when offered. But still nothing to compare with that first love affair with Betsy.

Then, in the late summer of 1978, serendipity struck again.

Arlene

It was Labor Day weekend at my cousin Jerry's, down on the farm. Well, not exactly The Farm. The real farm was next door, over the hill. Jerry had bought a seventy-acre piece of land that was originally owned by Joe and Earl McMahon, first cousins of Bill McMahon, owner of The Farm, the place where I vicariously grew up and where I often return to in my imagination. More about The Farm perhaps later.

Jerry had converted what was originally a working farm (in the 19th-century sense) into a weekend retreat. From the beams and planks of the old barn, long collapsed, he and his kids had constructed a sturdy, if not elegant, cabin that for the most part kept out the elements. Over the years, he added electricity, insulation, plumbing, and a Franklin stove. By 1978, it was pretty much in its finished state.

The big three summer weekends, Memorial Day, 4th of July, and Labor Day, were usually open house to an assortment of guests, most of whom were Jerry's friends, or his brother and sister's friends, and family. Arlene was Jerry's wife's younger sister. She had been married to a doctor, had seven children with him, and was either divorced or soon to become so. Prior to 1978, I had met her once or twice at The Farm or possibly at Jerry's place. However, in the summer of 1978, she was a frequent guest at Jerry's. That summer, I ran into her at least once prior to Labor Day. I was a frequent visitor at The Farm, and I usually made a point to stop in and see Jerry if I thought he might be there, which was just about every weekend. It was a three-mile walk from The Farm through woods and fields, or you could get there by car in about ten minutes by taking the road.

Arlene and I were instantly attracted to each other when we first saw each other that summer of 1978. I remember all of us sitting outside, on the left side of Jerry's cabin. We were in lawn chairs, arranged in a rough semicircle, with various drinks in our hands. Arlene would say something and I would laugh, or I would say something and she would laugh, each of us furtively glancing at the other to see what effect our words had. She had an impish, mischievous smile, playfully and innocently flirtatious, which she used with reckless abandon. I don't recall having any sexual thoughts about her at that point. All I could think of was how much I enjoyed being in her company. From that point on, whenever I visited The Farm (which had always been every two or three weeks), I hoped that I would run into her again.

The big weekends at Jerry's were always camping weekends. This was because there wasn't enough room in the cabin for many more than Jerry's own family, which comprised a wife, eight children, and a dog. The other thirty or so people would be spread about the vicinity in tents. That weekend, Arlene had brought only her two youngest boys, who spent most of the weekend playing with their cousins (Jerry's younger kids) and the various other children who were there with their parents.

I'm not sure when I arrived or who, if anyone, came with me. My parents, who when I was young had spent considerable time at The Farm, staying overnight frequently, did not visit The Farm as much as I did any more. Most likely I came alone, bringing my umbrella tent and sleeping bag, arriving early Friday evening just before dark. I didn't know whether Arlene would be there, but I had pretty good reason to believe she would, just as I was hoping she thought that I would. At any rate, whether it was Friday night or Saturday, I established contact with her immediately and remained with her more or less constantly until early Sunday evening, when most of the guests left for home. Of course, I didn't spend the night with her or engage in any physical affection, but it was obvious (perhaps to everyone, although I was unaware of anyone else's presence, let alone observations) that we wanted to be with each other as much as possible. Usually, in the early stages of a relationship, one tends to hang back a bit, not wishing to smother the other person, thus putting out the fire before it has a chance to get started. In this case, however, there was every indication that she wanted me to be with her; and I did not hesitate to oblige. Every moment spent with her was pure joy.

The only cloud over the weekend came on Sunday afternoon, when we realized that the party would soon be coming to an end. Who could have predicted that the weekend would have gone so well? A solution quickly materialized. Although Arlene had promised her family she would be home for Labor Day, there was nothing to prevent her from throwing a party herself. With my enthusiastic encouragement, she announced to everyone that they were invited to her house the following afternoon for a pool party. At that point, we would have been perfectly happy if no one showed up but ourselves; but, in fact, most of the weekend campers did come. It turned out to be a great party—one could even say memorable.

I showed up in the early afternoon, towel and bathing suit in hand, ready for anything. A few people were already there, and the rest gradually drifted in over the next couple of hours. It was as if the party at The Farm had been transplanted, *en masse,* to Arlene's back yard. I don't think I made my intention to be with Arlene as obvious as I had on Saturday and Sunday: I divided my time equally among the pool, the back yard, and the barbecue grill, where I assumed the role of principal chef.

In the evening, after everyone had eaten, many of us went inside and started to play parlor games. Just as people had gradually filtered in to the party, they began to filter out. I was determined to be the last to leave, and Arlene sensed this. Perhaps the remaining guests did, too. It must have been close to midnight when the last guest, other than myself, did leave. After all, the following day was a work day for most. By this time, all of Arlene's kids were either in bed or otherwise accounted for (some were with their father).

After we were alone, we continued the pretense of playing some game or other, but eventually we started hugging and kissing. Things got pretty intense; but, incredibly, neither of us had any serious intention of going any farther, as if to do so would be to spoil the magic of the whole thing. At one point, Arlene said, "We're not going to have intercourse tonight." She meant this not as a rejection—and I understood.

We came up for air, so to speak, and started talking about our pasts. I described one or two of my disappointing love affairs, and she described her marriage. This went on for an hour or so, and then we started necking again. Finally, shortly before dawn, we decided that I'd better go. The kids would be up soon, and explaining my presence might prove awkward.

Over the coming weeks, I visited Arlene a few more times. It became apparent, however, that despite how much we liked each other, anything more than a friendship was impractical. She was forty-four, I was thirty-two. The age difference was not important, but our life experiences were. I was temperamentally unsuited to be with children,[2] and I think Arlene knew that.

Also, as I suspected at the time and got confirmation of later, Jerry and his wife were vehemently opposed to any romantic relationship I might have with Arlene. I'm not sure why. Perhaps it was because Jerry and his wife, being *strict* Catholics, were opposed to Arlene's divorce in the first place. After all, the Catholic Church did not permit or recognize divorce. The only legitimate way to dissolve a marriage was annulment, which was a decree saying the marriage was never valid in the first place! Arlene had actually tried to go that route; but when her parish priest explained what an annulment was, she balked. What the annulment said, in effect, was that the marriage never existed—so how do you explain the existence of seven children? Aside from this, there were the bureaucratic and financial hassles of getting an annulment: a process designed, I'm sure, to discourage people from using it.

---

[2] Not because I was a child molester or anything like that. It was just that I never wanted children of my own, let alone anyone else's. I'm not sure why—perhaps I was overwhelmed by the responsibility of being a parent.

Lastly, there was Mike. Mike was a man in his late forties or early fifties who was also going through a divorce. He, too, had children. Mike was very much in love with Arlene, and I'm sure she was fond of him. In the end, Mike and Arlene got married. As a matter of practicality, it was a better match than Arlene and I would have been. But we both knew that what we had experienced, however briefly, was something unique and wonderful, never perhaps to be duplicated on this earth. It was a treasure to be hidden away, opened only on special occasions, and then put carefully back. There were no regrets on my part or hers.

In retrospect, my love affairs with Betsy and Arlene, as well as my friendships with Phil and others, prove a point which has been demonstrated over and over again in my life but which I have only recently been able to comprehend: authentic relationships between people just *happen*; they can't be contrived. In this sense, they are like epiphanies, which are both fabulous and frustrating. They must be stumbled upon, like an old shoe in the dark—not sought in the conscious light of day.

So my advice is: don't go looking for love or friendship. Find something you like to do; do it; and friendship, maybe even love, will find *you*.

Cynara

I would like to close this chapter with a detailed discussion of an old movie, one of my favorites, called *Cynara,* released in 1932, starring Ronald Colman, Kay Francis, Phyllis Barry, and Henry Stephenson. I doubt if 1 percent of the people in this country have heard of this movie, or even its stars, two of whom (Ronald Colman and Kay Francis) were headliners in their day.

Today, *Cynara* would probably be called a soap opera, though this term may not have been used in 1932. The plot is characteristic of a soap opera, but its treatment of the subject is not. People under the age of 60 would probably laugh at its period dialogue; that is, if they could understand it at all. But it is a wonderful movie, worth struggling with, full of love, humor, passion, and most of all dignity. I think it is one of the most truly Christian movies ever made. I realize that some of you readers are not Christians, but I would like to think that many of the Christian themes presented in this movie (sin, suffering, forgiveness, and redemption) are universally understood.

The title is from a character in a poem by the 19th century decadent poet Ernest Dowson. The poem, which describes a man's inability to get over a lost love (named Cynara), closes each of its four stanzas with the memorable line:

I have been faithful to thee, Cynara! in my fashion.

The story centers in an adulterous love affair between prominent English lawyer Jim Warlock (Colman) and shop girl Doris Lea (Barry), whom he meets in a restaurant after his wife Clemency (Francis) and her younger sister depart for Venice on a holiday designed to protect the sister from a potentially disastrous romance at home. This sort of thing would be incomprehensible today, just as would an extended trip to Aunt Millie's in Iowa to wait out an unexpected pregnancy.

The key points to remember, however, are:

- Jim is still very much in love with Clemency (and she with him), even after seven years of marriage.
- He's terribly upset by his wife's sudden and unexpected departure, since he had made elaborate plans to celebrate their anniversary.
- Jim's first meeting with Doris is accidental, and he has no intention of seeing her again.
- The second and fateful meeting is entirely arranged by Jim's friend Tring (Stephenson), whose motives are unclear.
- Even then, Jim is extremely reluctant to continue the association; but he and Doris seemed to be propelled by some irresistible force.

The story is told in flashback, with Jim and Clemency in Naples waiting for Jim's boat to depart for South Africa, where he hopes to reconstitute his life after a devastating scandal in London, in which Doris commits suicide because she can't have Jim. In the short time before his embarkation (presumably alone), Jim tries again to explain to Clemency what happened. The narrative begins in Jim's office, where Jim's friend Tring is congratulating him on a brilliant performance in court.[3] Jim, however, is more concerned about the

---

[3] I had originally intended to include this and two other conversations in the book. I have a copy of the movie *Cynara* in my personal collection, which I recorded from a PBS broadcast many years ago. I transcribed these conversations verbatim from the movie soundtrack, hoping that it would provide the reader with a better sense of the setting, the characters, and their feelings. However, I was unable to get permission from the production company to use the actual conversations. To my knowledge, the movie has not been shown again on television (or anywhere else). But I strongly urge the reader to see it if the opportunity arises.

anniversary celebration he has been planning for himself and Clemency. Tring, on the other hand, is unimpressed by Jim's marital bliss. He good-naturedly chides Jim on not paying more attention to his legal career. After all, Tring says, Jim is becoming a very important person. But Tring fears that Jim is settling into a comfortable routine, that he's becoming smug. As a prominent and influential lawyer, Jim should be entitled to a few diversions, things that will add color and spice to his life. In other words, without actually saying so, Tring is encouraging Jim to take a mistress. In the spirit of what he considers to be Tring's harmless kidding, Jim responds by rhetorically asking whether he should take the kitchen maid to Paris for the weekend. The scene ends with Jim inviting Tring over to his house for a cocktail before he and Clemency go out to celebrate their anniversary. Jim facetiously suggests that the King should knight him for his marital fidelity. Tring agrees that Jim deserves some kind of reward for all that he's missing and says that he will drink a toast to the last of the virtuous men. Tring laughingly calls Jim a Puritan as they walk out the door.

This exchange is fascinating to me for a number of reasons. In the first place, consider the time period when the movie was made, which was probably late 1931 or early 1932. This was prior to the full implementation of the Production Code (created in 1930, but not put into strict effect until July 1, 1934), which placed both general and specific limits on what could be shown in American films. For example:

The sanctity of the institution of marriage and the home shall be upheld. Pictures shall not infer that low forms of sex relationships are the accepted or the common thing.

The above conversation, however, strongly suggests that marital infidelity, "playing around," is definitely "a common thing." In fact, the faithful husband appears to be something of an anachronism ("the last of the virtuous men"). Even though the setting of this film is the English upper class, the film was made in America for consumption by American audiences, which is a good indication that the marital practices described in this film were prevalent throughout society. This is the reason that the pre-Production Code films provide an accurate picture of American life and mores during the 1920s and early 1930s.

Note, however, that Tring does not attack the institution of marriage. He is merely questioning Jim's strict adherence to its rules. Contrast this with our own time, where marriages dissolve at the drop of a hat. I'm not sure which is better: to preserve marriage as an institution at all costs, while allowing the partners considerable latitude in their behavior; or to insist on perfect marriage, where any failure results in divorce. Based on the evidence accumulated over the past 40 years or so, it would seem that, from the standpoint of social stability at least, it's better to preserve a marriage whenever possible, especially when children are involved. Children are resilient, I know; but growing up is tough enough already, even when all the home conditions are right.

Finally, there is the character Tring himself. When I first saw the movie, I was shocked by Tring's attitude. He seems like such a kindly old man, sort of a grandfather or Dutch uncle. And yet he playfully rebukes Jim for not cheating on his wife, as if it were expected of a man in his position. Later in the film, after Jim and Doris have become hopelessly entangled, the situation is made impossible by Clemency's return. Jim realizes that he must end the affair with Doris and asks Tring's advice.

Tring says that Jim must end the affair, even though Doris will suffer. The fact that Jim is a compassionate and caring man will only make it more difficult for him to do what must be done. There's no such thing as letting a person down easy, since the breakup itself is so painful that nothing can alleviate it. Speaking from his own experience, Tring says that extramarital love affairs start out with people thinking that they can manage things. Initially, they agree to see each other only at certain times and under certain circumstances. Eventually, however, they lose control of the situation. One or both parties can no longer abide by the original rules. The stakes get higher and higher until it becomes an all-or-nothing game. Expressing both wisdom and cynicism, Tring extends his critique of human love to the institution of marriage, when he shrewdly observes that women hope marriage *will* change the husbands and that men hope marriage *won't* change the wives. Inevitably, he says, both are disappointed.

This conversation takes place as Jim is composing a note to Doris, canceling their appointment for the afternoon and telling her that they can no longer see each other. Jim dispatches a messenger to deliver the note, who unknowingly passes Doris in the street on his way to her flat. Presumably, she discovers the note after returning from the abortive meeting with Jim and then, tragically, commits suicide after confronting the hopelessness of her situation. One of the most poignant moments ever recorded on film occurs shortly after, when Jim is informed of Doris's death by a police officer—in the presence of his wife and Doris's roommate, who had come to see Jim on Doris's behalf. The look on Jim's face is one of genuine horror and anguish, a truly memorable piece of acting on Colman's part. The editing is equally brilliant, as the scene cuts quickly to the equally horrified look on Clemency's face and then back to Jim. None of the rank, manipulative sentimentality so prevalent in today's films.

I had always thought of the 1930s as such a conservative, morally upright period—probably because most of the movies shown on TV in the 1950s were made *after* the Production Code went into effect. The Astaire-Rogers musicals are a good example of this. Consider their first film, *Flying Down to Rio* (1933). Ginger is blatantly sexy, especially in the opening number, "Music Makes Me" (a play on words?). One of the girls in the audience, on spotting the darkly beautiful Dolores Del Rio, a Brazilian heiress, rhetorically complains: "What do these South Americans have below the Equator that we don't?"

Gene Raymond, who along with Dolores are the nominal stars of the picture, is immediately captivated and arranges to have her fly with him in his private plane down to her home in Rio de Janeiro, where he, Fred and Ginger, and the rest of the band are scheduled to play. Once airborne, Gene fakes an emergency, which allows him the opportunity to land the plane on a "deserted" beach (actually, it's next to a golf course), where they are "forced" to spend the night. Despite her protestations of virtue and his reservations about taking advantage of the situation, it's obvious that they will make love. The rest of the movie is similarly explicit (compared to its own time, but not, of course, to ours).

Contrast this film with *Shall We Dance?* (1936), where much of the fun comes from the confusion surrounding Fred and Ginger's "marriage." At the hotel where Fred and Ginger are staying in adjoining suites, the Floor Manager, the wonderful Eric Blore, keeps changing the locks on the connecting door because he's not sure whether they're really married (which would, of course, entitle them to have access to each other's rooms). Then there's the roller skating number in the park, where an old Irish cop, upon overhearing what appears to be Fred's refusal to marry Ginger (shotgun style, perhaps?), frowns and then, when Fred appears to be running out of excuses, suggests that they go to New Jersey, where it will be easier to get a license and get married quickly. Finally, there's the bedroom scene, where Ginger's agent Arthur (Jerome Cowan) arranges to have a Ginger-manikin photographed in bed with Fred to convince Ginger's old boy friend that she's really married to Fred. A great comedy, in the best screwball tradition, with the added magic of the Astaire-Rogers singing and dancing. The key point, though, is that despite all of the shenanigans, mostly the result of innocent misunderstandings, the rules of sexual propriety have been scrupulously observed. No suggestion of any "low forms of sex relationships."

But getting back to Tring. I guess the best description of him is the one given by himself, toward the end of the movie, where he persuades Clemency to forgive Jim and join him on the boat. He refers to himself as Mephistopheles, diabolical tempter in the Faust legend. This would seem to be apt, since Tring devises an elaborate scheme to have Jim meet up with Doris again, even after Jim had told Tring he had no intention of seeing her after their accidental encounter in the restaurant. This point is underscored by Jim's tearing up the paper on which Doris had written her address and phone number and throwing the pieces out the window of a cab, despite Tring's encouragement to pursue her.

This raises the question of Tring's motives. Does he really believe that an extramarital affair would be good for Jim, adding some needed color and variety to his life; or is he really the Devil incarnate, trying to seduce Jim and send him down the path to perdition? Well, maybe only temporarily; for it is Tring who ultimately saves the marriage by appearing, as a *deus ex machina*, just in time to induce Clemency (true to her name) to reconcile with Jim.

The final part of the flashback sequence is the inquest, where Jim must testify concerning the circumstances surrounding Doris's suicide. True to his gentleman's code, Jim protects Doris's reputation at the expense of his own by implying that he was her first lover when in fact she had had at least one other. This would have made a significant difference in the eyes of the jury and the presiding magistrate, who sternly tells Jim that, regrettably, he cannot be held *criminally* responsible for Doris's death. The scene ends with the magistrate's condemnatory remarks ringing through the court, which continue into the present as Jim repeats them, placing his hands over his ears as if to silence the unrelenting censure.

Hard on the heels of Jim's departure for the boat, Tring arrives. Assuming that Tring is here to see Jim, Clemency informs him that Jim has just left. She is surprised when Tring says that he wants to see *her*. Expressing obvious displeasure with Tring for being the cause of her and Jim's troubles, she tells him that they don't have much to say to each other. Acknowledging his own responsibility, while dismissing the uselessness of arguments about who's to blame for what, Tring quickly changes the focus to Jim. Although Jim has suffered greatly, Tring asks Clemency not to pity Jim but instead to imagine what her life would be without him. He also raises the possibility, though slight, of Jim's committing suicide by jumping off the boat before it reaches South Africa. Clemency, obviously moved by Tring's words, stares off into space as the scene shifts to the pier, where an exuberant crowd is shouting "Bon Voyage" to the passengers waving from the boat. The next thing we see is Jim slowly, almost aimlessly, moving along the rail, alternating his gaze between shore and deck, as though looking for something he doesn't expect to find. Suddenly his face illuminates, as he spots Clemency further down the rail. What follows is one of the great reconciliation scenes in movie history, all the more remarkable because it is accomplished in complete silence, with gestures and expressions telling the whole story.

And so we come full circle: Tring, who is directly responsible for the whole sordid mess, ends up as the savior. He is both tempter and redeemer.

Cynara can be viewed simply as a soap opera, albeit a classy one. Perhaps this is all the author intended. But *Cynara* has always struck a philosophical and religious chord in me. Specifically, it touches profoundly on two universal human themes: suffering and God. Human suffering, from the time of Job to the present, has confounded philosophers and theologians. The basic problem is the reconciliation of suffering, especially of the innocent, with a benevolent God. In our own time, the Holocaust is the prime example of this. How could God make a world in which children are systematically tortured and killed? How could He ignore their cries?

Cynara may provide a clue. Jim and Clemency were

both good people. Neither had ever been unfaithful, and they were very much in love. Their only conceivable fault may have been smugness, but there is little suggestion of this in the movie. Perhaps Clemency took Jim for granted by going off to Venice with her sister, but she had a good reason. Maybe Jim was being selfish by wanting her to stay and celebrate their anniversary. Certainly, neither of them did anything to warrant their subsequent suffering. Tring, supposedly Jim's best friend, comes along and, almost in the spirit of a schoolboy prank, gets Jim involved in a love affair which he tries to his best to avoid. The results are devastating. Doris dies, Jim's reputation is ruined, and Clemency is left with no alternative but to let Jim go alone into exile in South Africa. One gets the feeling that all the principals in this movie, except Tring, have been unfairly treated.

There is a wonderful old proverb (I'm paraphrasing the original German): "What does not kill me makes me stronger." Human suffering, despite its unpleasantness, is a great teacher, though the message is not always or immediately apparent. What was learned from this movie? Perhaps that love is the most important thing we have. There is a hint that Jim and Clemency's happiness is at least partially based on the superficial perfection of their life: Jim is very successful, they appear to have plenty of money, and both occupy a favorable position in society. In the end, much of this is taken away. What is left? Their love, gloriously reaffirmed on the boat to South Africa, with Tring beaming his approval from the pier. After all, wasn't it Tring who said that Jim was becoming smug and that he needed something to add color and excitement to his life?

The other theme suggested by *Cynara* is the fact that

suffering appears to be inextricably woven into the fabric of human life. In other words, this is the way God designed the world. Jim Warlock, "the last of the virtuous men," didn't seem to be in need of reform or even enlightenment. He was a genuinely good person, much like Job in the Old Testament. However, like Job, he is made to suffer for no apparent reason. The same, of course, could be said of Jesus Christ. But Christ suggested an answer to this problem by linking human suffering, symbolized by the Cross, to resurrection and eternal life. In the movie, Jim emerges from his ordeal a sadder but wiser man. Though stripped of his position and probably much of his wealth, things that he may have been attached to as a prominent London barrister, he realizes that Clemency's love and forgiveness are all that really matter. And if you believe, with Saint John the Evangelist,[4] that God is love, then this is the best way we humans can experience Him on this earth.

---

[4] 1 John 4:7–8.

5. Living

There's an old song, written in 1931, which goes like this:

People are queer.
They're always crowing,
Scrambling and rushing about.
Why don't they stop some day
And address themselves this way:

Why are we here?
Where are we going?
It's time that we found out.
We're not here to stay.
We're on a short holiday.

Life is just a bowl of cherries.
Don't take it serious.
It's too mysterious.

You work, you slave, you worry so.
But you can't take your dough
When you go go go.
So keep repeating: it's the berries.
The strongest oak must fall.
The sweet things in life
To you were just loaned.
So how can you lose
What you've never owned?

Life is just a bowl of cherries.
So live and laugh at it all.[1]

This song became popular not long after the stock market crash of October 1929, which historically marks the beginning of the Great Depression. It certainly doesn't reflect the spirit of the 1920s, the Era of Wonderful Nonsense, which itself was a reaction to the First World War.

World War I is mostly forgotten now. All but a handful of its participants are dead. But I believe it is the seminal event of the 20th Century, and its reverberations can be felt to this day in places like Bosnia and the Middle East.

The First World War shattered man's vision of hope in the future, based to a great extent on rapid technological progress, when that technology was employed for diabolical purposes on the battlefield. While Europe suffered both spiritually and materially from the nightmare of 1914–1918, America emerged relatively unscathed. In fact, America had

---

[1] "Life is Just a Bowl of Cherries," lyrics by Lew Brown and music by Ray Henderson, 1931.

profited from the war. Relatively few of its citizens had experienced the horrors of the war, and mostly toward the end, when the doughboys tipped the scales in favor of the Entente. Many of those who had seen action, either as combatants or medics, remained in Europe, becoming the Lost Generation. America meanwhile, flushed with confidence and brimming with economic power, was in a party mood. Enter the Roaring Twenties.

The stock market crash of 1929 and the subsequent Great Depression affected the confidence of Americans in much the same way as the First World War did for Europeans. Even those Americans who hadn't been devastated by the Crash soon found that their jobs, and hence their lives, were no longer secure. This realization is perfectly reflected in the song quoted above.

During good economic times, like the recent 1990s, we tend to forget just how precarious our human existence is. At the height of the boom, some people even thought that we had finally figured out a way to repeal the business cycle. But the scary fact is that ever since the mass exodus from the family farm in the early 20th century, almost everyone in this country is totally dependent on the business and commercial system. Apart from that, most of us would find it very difficult if not impossible to make a living for ourselves, even if we knew how.

And so I return to a question posed at the outset of this book: what are we, both individually and collectively, supposed to do with our lives?

Leaving aside for the moment the notion of an ultimate purpose, which I will return to later, I believe there are three fundamentally worthwhile things to do in this life:

91

- Knowing
- Loving
- Creating

Knowing

Man has a basic urge to know. This runs the gamut from mere curiosity to science, philosophy, and theology.

In its pure form, without regard for possible exploitation, the quest for knowledge is a noble enterprise. As far as we know, it is unique to man. However, before we get too deeply into our discussion, it may be helpful to make a crucial distinction.

I will use the word *knowledge* to mean facts: information about reality that we can verify with our senses or reasoning faculty. This would include such things as historical data, mathematical formulas, or even scientific theories, such as General Relativity or Quantum Mechanics.

I will use the term *wisdom* to mean an understanding of subjects that are not quantifiable or describable by mathematical laws. This would include, for example, the study of human behavior and emotions or an inquiry into the nature of being.

Man has achieved incredible results from his pursuit of knowledge. This is perhaps most evident in the fields of science and technology. However, in the area of wisdom, the results have not been so good.

This dichotomy between knowledge and wisdom has proven disastrous for mankind. War is the most obvious example of this; but the First World War is particularly instructive. Between the Franco-Prussian War of 1870–1871 and the First World War of 1914–1918, Europe had experienced an era of almost uninterrupted peace. Even the Franco-Prussian War was a relatively short-lived and small-scale affair, fought by professional armies in the traditional way. The American Civil War of 1861–1865, though it involved large armies, was still a pre-technological conflict. The high casualty rates were more a function of the numbers involved and the primitive medical services.

Perhaps the most tragic thing about the First World War was that it was entirely unnecessary. I suppose the same thing could be said about most wars. The end result is usually not worth the human suffering, the expenditure of money, and the socio-political upheaval which inevitably follows. However, there simply was no compelling reason for any of the combatants to go to war in 1914. Understandably, Austria was upset with Serbia over the assassination of Archduke Francis Ferdinand; but Serbia all but capitulated in the face of Austria's demands. As soon as Austria made the fateful decision to punish Serbia with military action, the fate of Europe was sealed. The system of alliances and mobilization plans that had been forged over decades automatically kicked into operation at the first sign of trouble. The Kaiser and Czar Nicholas had some inkling of the disaster to come and frantically sent notes to each other, hoping to avoid the confrontation. The General Staffs, however, insisted on mobilizing their armies to prevent the other side from gaining an advantage. Once this happened, the game was over. Mobilization plans had been devised with precise timetables that could not be altered.

The only chance for peace was if England, the only one

of the major European powers which was not obligated by treaty to enter the war automatically, could somehow play the role of mediator. But when Germany invaded Belgium, which the Schlieffen Plan required, England was honor-bound by tradition to defend Belgian neutrality. With frightening swiftness, Austria's punitive expedition against Serbia had turned into a World War.

Is anyone to blame for this cataclysm? Could it have been prevented? Certainly there were individuals in all the warring countries who realized the folly of what was taking place. For the most part, these were the intellectuals, the purveyors of wisdom. Unfortunately, their influence did not extend to the level of government, which is a collective representation of the ordinary citizens' aspirations and fears.

In my opinion, Austria bears most of the responsibility for what happened. Perhaps the Emperor Franz Joseph was too old and feeble to reign in his bellicose diplomats and generals. Perhaps he lacked the wisdom necessary to do so. At any rate, it's doubtful whether the war could have been prevented, given the prevailing spirit of the time, which emphasized national pride, military prowess, and a profound distrust of other nations. Millions had to die before the collective wisdom of mankind advanced.

This leads us to an interesting difference between knowledge and wisdom. Knowledge proceeds automatically, instinctively; while wisdom is gained fitfully, grudgingly, sometimes only after intense suffering. A League of Nations would have been unthinkable before the First World War; afterwards, it seemed the only practicable way for mankind to avert self-destruction.

Another difference is that knowledge is easily transferable, whereas wisdom is not. Knowledge can be recorded in books, computers, or other media and then recovered later with no degradation of content. The truth of the Pythagorean Theorem is as evident today as when it was first discovered over 2,000 years ago. Modern schoolboys learn Euclid's geometry the same as their ancestors did in ancient Greece. Not necessarily with wisdom. For example, the rules of ethical behavior, which embody the accumulated wisdom of society, may be learned but not understood. A man may know that extramarital sex is wrong; but until he experiences firsthand its devastating effects on his own or another's marriage, he may regard its prohibition as merely an arbitrary rule.

Which leads us to the fascinating question of whether there is any connection between what man *does* and what man *knows*. Knowledge, as we have defined it above, would appear to be morally neutral. In other words, knowing the General Theory of Relativity does not induce us to treat people in any particular way. However, knowing that the Fifth Race at Saratoga is fixed might induce us to place a bet on a particular horse. On the other hand, that same knowledge might induce us to alert law-enforcement authorities to prevent people from being cheated. In this situation, the mere knowledge of an event or a condition does not induce us to decide on a course of action. Rather, it is our value system, which can only be found in the realm of wisdom.

In Plato's *Dialogues* (*Meno*, 88e–89a), Socrates concludes:

So we may say in general that the goodness of non-spiritual assets depends on our spiritual character, and the goodness of that on wisdom. This argument shows that the advantageous element must be wisdom, and virtue, we agree, is advantageous; so that amounts to saying that virtue, either in whole or in part, is wisdom.[2]

How is a value system formed? Certainly one component is the accumulation of experience, which is knowledge of events and their consequences. But this is not sufficient. As we stated earlier, mere knowledge of facts is morally neutral. It does not compel a person to do one thing as opposed to another. The other component—and this is the key component in value formation—is human compassion.

If there is one thing which gives me hope for the future of mankind, it is compassion, which I will define as the ability to feel another's pain, *and then want to alleviate it,* as though the pain were one's own. When you think about it, it's hard to account for. We're all familiar with the maternal instinct, which exists in both man and animals, but this is different. It seems to run counter to the basic instinct for survival, which would prevent one from being concerned about anyone but oneself. In fact, compassion is so strong among some people that they are willing to place their own existence in jeopardy to help another. And, I'm happy to say, based on my own observations (which obviously encompass only a minuscule part of human experience), that compassion exists to some degree or other in all but the most pathological of human beings. And so, when one combines the knowledge of human actions and their consequences with one's concern for others (compassion), a positive (ethical) value system can emerge. The ultimate

---

[2] *The Collected Dialogues of Plato,* ed. by Edith Hamilton and Huntington Cairns (Princeton, Princeton University Press, 1989), p. 374.

expression of this is the Golden Rule, which enjoins people to treat each other the way they would like to be treated themselves; or, in Christian terms, love thy neighbor as thyself.

Knowing, therefore, is eminently worthwhile. However, in order to survive, we must be seekers of wisdom as well as of knowledge.

Loving

Love means many things. Considered only as it relates to one's feelings toward other *beings* (as opposed to the love of some *thing,* such as money or fame), I can think of several distinct kinds of love:

- Sexual
- Romantic
- Maternal
- Familial
- Fraternal
- Christian
- Divine

Let me describe each with a paragraph or two.

Sexual love is one of the fundamental forces of nature. It is the method by which both human and non-human species reproduce themselves, thus ensuring their survival. However, it is only in man that sex is problematical. This is because any relationship between two people can have moral consequences. In other words, human interactions involve optional behaviors which may be judged in relation to accepted standards. For example, the act of sexual union is natural and universal. It has the same meaning, in terms of its biological purpose, in all times and in all cultures. However, the behaviors preceding and following it are not. They may differ in accordance with the needs and customs of society.

In our own time and culture, there is a debate about those behaviors. Some people want to retain the traditional norms, in which the man and woman have sexual union only after a marriage ceremony which requires them to remain together for the rest of their lives. This formula is rooted not only in religious tradition, but also in biological, economic, and social necessities. Since all of these limitations have now been eliminated, many people are wondering if it's time for a paradigm shift (to borrow Thomas Kuhn's terminology). Human procreation could now resemble the situation in the animal kingdom, where the male's function would be simply to impregnate the female, who would then assume sole responsibility for rearing the child. The female, freed from any economic dependence on the male or society, would be spared the potential problems associated with marriage (and so would the child). Of course, technology has made it possible to dispense with the reproductive function of sex altogether, thus allowing sex to be used solely for the pleasure it provides.

Romantic love is not the same as sexual love, though many people would assume that it is. The difference is in the state of mind of the lover. This is best illustrated by example. Consider the case of the adolescent boy or girl who has a crush on a teacher. If the boy or girl is sexually inexperienced, the attraction to the teacher is usually based on a combination of looks, personality, dress, etc. The teacher becomes an ideal man or woman, representing the hopes and dreams of the youthful admirer. Sexual contact would destroy such a vision rather than fulfill it. Contrast this with a middle-aged divorced man in a singles bar, five or six martinis into the evening, staring at a voluptuous blonde sitting, legs crossed, three stools away. Chances are he's not waxing poetic.

It would be a mistake, however, to think that romantic love is just for the immature. It may come to anyone at any time. It is usually unsolicited and unanticipated. The key point is the feeling that the beloved evokes in the lover. The excitement, the magic, may be so intense that sex is anticlimactic.

Maternal or motherly love is instinctive and requires no explanation.

Familial or family love, as between siblings or between parents and children or grandchildren, is natural, though not perhaps instinctive.

Fraternal love is friendship. Like romantic love, it is unsolicited and unanticipated. It develops gradually, imperceptibly. Most often, it is rooted in a chance confluence of circumstances: being together at the same time and place or having a common interest. This why so many friendships originate at school, play, or work. Sometimes, friends are made through other friends.

Friendship differs from romance in three important ways. In the first place, friendship is almost never consciously sought, while romance frequently is. This is perhaps the biggest problem with romance: one person is "in love," while the other isn't. There is a strong temptation for the person in love, who senses that the object of his affection doesn't reciprocate, to try to induce a change of heart. Sometimes this works, but one has to be careful. It's very easy for the process of winning a lover to become a quest, a mission, a crusade, in which the struggle itself becomes more important than the outcome. This has happened to me several times, once with disastrous consequences. On the other hand, take the case of President Harry S. Truman, who steadfastly pursued Bess Truman for many years before she finally consented to marry him. Harry must have known that Bess was the only woman for him, and he must also have known that she felt the same way about him, even though she couldn't give him any clear signal, owing primarily to the opposition of her domineering mother (who still looked down on Harry even after he became President) and the fact that for many years Harry didn't have any substantial means of supporting her (and her mother). In the end, Harry took Bess's acceptance in stride, as though he knew it all along. In other words, he wasn't undone by success.

Another difference between friendship and romance is that friendship is seldom the object of conscious reflection, whereas romance is usually uppermost in our minds as something that must be cherished, nourished, or struggled with. This is especially true of friendship between males, who are usually embarrassed to talk about it, though this is changing somewhat, due to the increased sensitivity of people in general.

Thirdly, friendship has no ulterior motives (in contrast to a business acquaintance, for example). Romance often does, as in the case of a person pursuing another for the sheer excitement of it or out of some deep psychological need. Friends simply enjoy each other's company or just naturally gravitate toward each other, usually with no particular purpose in mind.

Christian[3] love is different from all the others mentioned so far. The five types of love discussed above have this much in common: they are based on the natural connections between people, physical and/or emotional. Christian love enjoins us to treat other people in the same way as we would treat ourselves or, better yet, as God would treat them. This may require us to go against our natural inclinations. For example, we may not like a particular person. However, if we found him lying on the road after an accident, we would be expected to care for him, just as if he were a family member. The key point is that Christian love does not demand that we like everybody or socialize with everybody. It simply means that we treat them as Christ would have.

Christian love is in some sense a duty, though there are certain rare individuals, like Mother Theresa of Calcutta, who have been able to transcend the obligatory aspect of Christian love and experience that most precious of all gifts: *divine* love. What this means, I believe, is that in the act of loving her fellow humans, Mother Theresa encountered God. In his First Letter, the Apostle John writes:

> God is love, and he who abides in love abides in God, and God abides in him.[4]

Love, no matter how you define it, is an eminently worthwhile human activity. Beginning with its purely physi-

---

[3] I use the term "Christian" because this type of love is associated with the teachings of Jesus Christ. I do not mean to imply that it is practiced *only* by Christians.
[4] 1 John 4:16.

cal form, sex, and proceeding up the ladder to its spiritual expression in Christian and divine love, we see that in some mysterious way, love may be the door to ultimate reality and meaning.

Creating

Creating may be another way to experience, or at least emulate, God.

When people think of the word *creation,* as it applies to human activity, they usually think of the artist: painter, sculptor, composer, or writer. But I believe that there are several other kinds of human endeavor that are encompassed by this word. All of these are different expressions of man's basic urge to engage in some form of meaningful activity, apart from knowing or loving, which produces a tangible result.

When anthropologists attempt to determine whether fossil remains represent human beings, one of the key criteria is whether there are tools or weapons among the bones. It would seem that man, by nature, is a maker or creator. Who can forget the opening scene in Stanley Kubrick's *2001: A Space Odyssey,* in which one of the apes uses a bone as a weapon in his fight with another ape? Is Kubrick suggesting that this was the critical moment in man's evolution, when the ape found that he could gain a tremendous advantage by employing a tool? The suggestion of this is very powerful, since the very next scene is that of a space station orbiting majestically to the strains of the "Blue Danube Waltz," a tribute not only to man's technological progress but to his artistic accomplishments as well.

And so the word *creation* applies to anyone who makes

something: the factory worker, the carpenter, the brickla
Of course, there are some types of factory work that can'
dignified as being creative: sweeping the floor, deliver
parts, etc. This type of activity is simply referred to as wo
or toil.

Some kinds of creative activity don't result in the mak
ing of a material object. One of the most obvious examples is
the entertainer: the singer, comedian, athlete, etc. The tangible result of this kind of activity is the feeling produced in the
audience: joy, laughter, wonder. Another example is the service professional: the doctor, lawyer, teacher, etc. The doctor's results are perhaps the most tangible, but who can
calculate the influence of a memorable teacher?

One of the prevailing misconceptions about the nature
of creative human activity concerns the motivation of the en-
trepreneur, the person who takes an idea and transforms it
into a business enterprise. Most people assume that the person's reason for doing this is money. Here we need to make a
distinction. Obviously, there are people whose *only* interest
is in making money. To them, a business venture is only a
means of accomplishing that goal. Therefore, the type of
business they're engaged in is immaterial. It could be anything from pornography to a pyramid scheme. Contrast this
type of individual with someone like George Eastman, the
man who did for photography what Henry Ford did for the
automobile.

From his early manhood, George Eastman was fascinated by photography. However, when he first started working with it, he was frustrated by the difficulties involved in
taking pictures. To give but one example: before you could
make an exposure, you had to coat a photographic plate with

the appropriate chemicals (the emulsion). Since these chemicals were sensitive to light, you had to have access to a dark room while doing the coating. This meant that if you were in the field, you had to carry an opaque tent with you. The other problem was that the coated plate had to be used immediately. If the chemicals dried, they would be useless. George Eastman became obsessed with the idea of making the picture-taking process both simple and convenient.

By day he toiled as a bank clerk, while at night he worked on the transformation of photography. The end result was the *Brownie* camera, which combined two technological breakthroughs: roll film and dry emulsion. Flexible film replaced the photographic plate. The film was coated with a dry emulsion at the factory and loaded into a light-tight camera. The film, which was mounted on a system of rollers, could be exposed and then advanced by the owner so that another exposure could be made. The emulsion was dry, so there was no need to use the film immediately. In all, the camera contained enough film for 100 exposures. When this was used up, the owner could simply return the camera to Kodak (George Eastman's company name), where the camera would be unloaded, the film processed, and the camera reloaded. The owner would receive back the finished photographs, along with the reloaded camera. Eastman's famous slogan was: "You push the button, we do the rest."

As a result of his invention, George Eastman became a fabulously wealthy man. However, during all those nights of feverish and dogged experimenting, I really don't think the thought of riches entered his mind. Like all true inventors, his concern was the fruition of an idea. The consequent material reward was essentially a by-product, never the goal.

I would like to conclude this section with another example of human creation (or more precisely, *pro*creation), one that is familiar to almost everyone and done by almost everyone: the birth of a child. This experience is so universal and instinctive that people don't regard it as a creative act. But perhaps it is the ultimate creative act, since the end result is a human being, a creature of infinite promise and possibility. For many people, condemned to labor at an unrewarding job or without any other meaningful occupation, this may be their one chance to participate in the creative process.

In fact, I would venture to guess that most of the sum total of human activity is in some way directed toward the creation and rearing of children. This provides the motivation for most of what we do, from the sublime to the silly. Unfortunately, many parents regard their children as little more than property, something to be nurtured and invested in, rather than human beings, whose attitudes and behaviors will be unleashed upon the world with inestimable consequences. Perhaps the creative energies of these people would be better directed toward some of the other activities discussed in this section.

6.   Success

Beth:	Other men lose their jobs, and what do *they* do? They find another job. You could go back to the rewrite desk.
Eddie:	No. I . . . I won't settle for that.
Beth:	Why won't you?
Eddie:	Hell, I was there 20 years ago.
Beth:	It pays a living, but you want more, is that it?
Eddie:	Yes, I want more and I'm getting it.
Beth:	But *how* are you getting it?
Eddie:	All I know is that if you don't have it you're a bum in anybody's book.

—The Harder They Fall

Introduction

Success in the 21st century (and the 20th, and the 19th, etc.) is commonly defined as the attainment of any or all of the following:

- Wealth
- Power
- Fame
- Romance

This chapter could be summed up as my rationalization for not achieving *any* of them.

Wealth

My interest in money is only as a means of survival. College taught me how to live on very little, and I've never lost the ability to do that.

My first real job after college was high school teaching, which in 1968 paid a minimal salary of $6500. Since I was living with my parents, this was plenty of money. For all practical purposes, I felt that I could buy whatever I wanted; and I didn't want very much. People then, as now, didn't go into teaching for the money. In my case, it was a natural career path, since I had originally intended to become a Jesuit priest, which would have meant teaching at the high school or college level. But in 1968, teaching high school had the additional advantage, at least in my part of the country, of providing me with a draft deferment, which was what I was most concerned about.

When my teaching career fizzled, I did end up in the military; but at least it was in a service of my choosing: the U.S. Coast Guard. The pay was ridiculously low, by civilian standards. However, when you consider that room, board, and medical expenses were completely paid for, it was not that bad of a deal. Also, the places where I was stationed over the next four years did not provide opportunities for lavish expenditures. Elizabeth City, North Carolina, for example, where I spent all but four months of my total enlistment, was a town of 30,000 or so inhabitants located in the northeast corner of the state about forty-five miles south of Norfolk,

Virginia. Norfolk itself was not that big; but it was part of a sprawling metropolitan area which included Hampton Roads, Newport News, and Virginia Beach. This was also home to the biggest naval complex on the entire east coast. There were Air Force and Marine units in the area, too.

Norfolk was just far enough away that it was inconvenient to go there during the week. Some of my friends went there on weekends to take advantage of the night life; but for me the big attraction was the huge Navy Exchange (PX), where you could buy almost anything at reduced prices. Locally, in Elizabeth City, there wasn't much to do in terms of entertainment. Like many southern towns, Elizabeth City was essentially dry. There was a bowling alley and a Holiday Inn where you could buy watered-down beer or "brown bag" it, which meant bringing your own wine or hard liquor, obtainable only at the state-run "package store." Regular beer was available at the supermarket, but you couldn't bring it to either of the establishments mentioned above. However, you could bring it to the drive-in, where my buddies and I (mostly students who were attending our training school for seven months) spent many a Friday or Saturday night spread out on blankets in the first row with our coolers and snacks.

Because the Coast Guard Base was a federal installation, it was exempt from the state liquor laws. Hence, there were three bars "on campus": one for lower-ranking enlisted men, one for higher-ranking enlisted men, and one for officers. Here you could buy any type of beer, wine, or mixed drink you wanted. The only problem was that guests (i.e., women) were not allowed—at least I never saw any. Maybe it was different for the other two clubs. I don't remember.

During my final year in the Coast Guard, I considered going back to school to get an advanced degree in English. This had been my original plan after graduating from college. I had been accepted into the Ph.D. program at the University of Virginia, where I would have been able to use my New York State Regents Teaching Fellowship (worth $2500 per year, a considerable sum at that time). I was all set to begin in the fall of 1968, when I fell victim to the draft lottery (my number was nineteen). Until the lottery was instituted in 1968, my local draft board had been granting deferments for graduate students. If I had graduated in 1967 as I was supposed to, I would have been fine (all my original classmates got deferments for graduate school). However, after the debacle of my sophomore year, where I managed to complete all my courses despite a horrendous start, I ended up taking junior year off—from Fordham, that is. I enrolled at a local college, which proved to be a disaster as well. However, the fact that I was still technically a student kept me out of the draft.

My plans to resume graduate school after the Coast Guard came to nought, though, when I checked around to see what the job market was for college English teachers. It turned out that projections for openings in the next four years were dismal. So, I abandoned the world of academic teaching once and for all and decided to try for a job in business or industry.

These were the days when you could send a resume to a company without any specific job or career goal in mind and let them decide where they could use you. If I had had any inclination to relocate to another part of the country, this would have been the perfect time to do it. Except for my junior year at the local college and the year and a half I spent teaching in high school, I had been living away from home for the last ten years and had gotten used to it. However, I had always made regular visits home and had no intention of living anywhere else, once my academic and military obligations were fulfilled.

In anticipation of my discharge from the Coast Guard in March of 1974, I sent my resume to Eastman Kodak Company in the fall of 1973.

In the mid 1970s, Kodak was the dominant employer in Rochester, New York (often called "The Kodak City"). It had over 50,000 workers then and would hire even more by the end of the decade. Kodak was the unquestioned leader in photography, employing over 125,000 people worldwide. Its success was due primarily to the simple idea of making photography as easy and inexpensive as possible ("You push the button, we do the rest"). Over the years, from the time when George Eastman revolutionized the picture-taking and development process with his Brownie camera and roll film, Kodak had introduced a steady stream of improvements, each one of which seemed to attract an increasing number of amateur picture takers. These were the kind of people who didn't want to fool with loading and setting up a 35mm camera, people who just wanted to point their camera at a subject, press a button, and be assured that their picture would turn out all right. Kodak satisfied this need perfectly.

Kodak's phenomenal success meant two things to me: (1) that I could probably find a job there and (2) that it would give me the wherewithal to find and marry the girl of my dreams. Money was not a consideration at all, except that it would be adequate to support a possible family. More about this later.

Kodak hired me as a technical writer, and I started work in March of 1974, exactly one week after leaving the Coast

Guard. I wasn't sure what a technical writer did, but it didn't matter. I would have accepted any job at that point. During my interview a few months earlier, I had noticed some very attractive women in the area where I would be working; and I was eager to get started in the corporate world.

Prior to my interview, I had never set foot inside a Kodak facility. I was thoroughly impressed with the whole operation, beginning with the letter inviting me for an interview. The personnel man who met me was friendly, knowledgeable, and well prepared. After directing me to the man who would be my boss, should I be hired, he informed me that he would be back later to pick me up at the conclusion of all my individual interviews with the various people in the department. A first-rate lunch was provided in the executive dining room, followed by a tour of my potential work area and conversations with some of my potential co-workers. Although I had no knowledge of photographic equipment, which is what I would be working on, I did have a solid background in electronics (thanks to Uncle Sam and the Coast Guard), so I was able to ask intelligent questions. The main thing I wanted to demonstrate was the fact that I was interested in what was going on, which apparently was some new computerized machine for printing negative images onto photographic paper. At the end of the day, which I thought had been orchestrated with military precision, the personnel man met me as promised and took me into his office for a feedback session. He asked me what I thought of the job; and even though I wasn't quite sure what I would be getting into, I tried to be as enthusiastic as possible without overdoing it. I wanted the job, whatever it was, and I think he knew it. We parted cordially, and he promised that I would be hearing from him shortly.

Within a week, I received a letter from Kodak at the Coast Guard base, offering me a position as technical writer at a yearly salary of $11,000. I was overjoyed. I immediately mailed in my acceptance letter. My opinion of Kodak was enhanced even more when they offered me some relocation money, knowing that I would be moving from North Carolina, even though my home was in Rochester.

And so began my long association with Kodak, which continues to this day. The company has changed drastically over the past thirty years. From a peak of over 60,000 in the early 1980's, the work force has shrunk to barely 20,000 today. The company's position in photography, which seemed unassailable in the mid-1970s, is under strong attack now from several companies, foreign and domestic. If I had worked continuously from my original hire date till now, my financial position would have been such that I could do whatever I wanted. But this was not to be. Although I received generous raises each of my first five years, so that my pay more than doubled by my sixth year, I was dissatisfied because I had not achieved the one thing I thought I wanted: romance. The money was great. I had enough to buy whatever I wanted, which wasn't much, and I managed to save a fair amount, which was to come in handy later when I left the company in the fall of 1979.

Over the next twenty-five years, during which I worked for Kodak again as well as several other companies, I continued to earn good money, though I never really tried to. The type of work I did paid well, and I just went along with it. Money fundamentally never interested me. I always had enough for my material needs, which were and are modest. I've left many jobs over the years, but never for money. It was always some vague dissatisfaction with my life, a quest for something which was perhaps unattainable.

It turned out that power, fame, and romance were to be equally unfulfilling.

Power

Power is the reason that people become scoutmasters, CEOs, or presidents. I think that I was even less interested in power than I was in money.

I'm one of those people who think of the glass as half empty rather than half full. The negative aspects of a thing always seem to outweigh the positive. One time when I was in high school, for example, my parish priest invited me to attend a dinner hosted by the local Optimists Club. I wasted no time in telling everyone I talked to that night that I couldn't understand why Father Geiger had brought me along, since I was a pessimist!

We all grow up wanting to be leaders. After all, they seem to have the most fun: telling people what to do (especially things you don't want to do yourself), being in the limelight, getting the attention of the pretty girls, etc.

In my opinion, the benefits of leadership and power are illusory. However, I also believe that leadership and power are absolutely essential to the running of any human enterprise. This leads me to the assertion that leaders are born, not made, and that no one should consciously and deliberately seek a position of power.

One of my favorite historical examples of this is the case of President Truman. I was born in 1945, just months after his accession to the presidency. I was seven years old when he left the White House in January of 1953, and I still have memories of his time in office. Two of the things that stand out in my mind are his daughter Margaret's singing career, including his response to one of her less kind critics, and his brisk morning walks. I also have a vague recollection of the furor generated by his firing of General MacArthur and Mac-Arthur's famous farewell speech before Congress.

What fascinates me about Truman is how he got there. He is the only president of the 20th century who never attended college. Prior to the First World War, he was a farmer—not a gentleman farmer, but a subsistence farmer, one who depended on the land for the barest essentials. After the war, he tried a number of things, most of which were unsuccessful. His big break came when he became county road commissioner, due to his wartime acquaintance with the son of Tom Pendergast, the most powerful Democratic boss in Missouri. Pendergast was so impressed with Truman's honesty, toughness, and fiscal efficiency that Truman was eventually selected to run in the U.S. Senate race, which he won. During the Second World War, in his second Senate term, he achieved moderate recognition for his efforts to curb waste and corruption in the awarding and administration of defense contracts. The truly amazing thing, though, was his selection as FDR's running mate for the 1944 election. Henry Wallace, the current vice-president, had to be dumped because his views were seen as too liberal—even radical. Other, better-known Democrats were rejected for strategic reasons. It was becoming obvious that a compromise candidate would have to be chosen, someone who could add geographic balance to the ticket without possessing any serious negatives. Truman met both these requirements, but there was one serious question: would he be able to handle the job of president, since it must have seemed obvious to everyone, including FDR, that FDR was a very sick man and probably wouldn't survive his term. I can't believe that Truman would have been considered, unless the Democratic Party bosses saw something in him that convinced them he was up to the task. In other words, Harry Truman must have had leadership qualities which were apparent to anyone who knew him.

Anyone who is part of a human organization, from a bowling team to a corporation, knows that certain individuals naturally emerge as leaders. Television commercials, which depict leaders as dynamic, positive, outgoing types like Tony Robbins, imply that anyone can be a leader, provided that he/she adopts the techniques taught in the home-study course you can purchase by calling the toll-free number at the bottom of your television screen. Corporations offer management seminars to their more ambitious employees. Self-help books discuss techniques for rising to the top. But the fact remains that leaders are born, not made, and the best ones don't even try. Such an assertion runs counter to our can-do culture, where everything is deemed possible, as long as we try hard enough. We don't like to be told that something is beyond our reach.

While I accept the notion that most human enterprises are amenable to our best efforts, I believe we have limitations that restrict, if not prevent, our ability to accomplish certain tasks. Another way of saying this is that we may not be the best person for a given job. For example, would anyone have been capable of leading the Normandy invasion, provided he/she had taken the appropriate management course? General George C. Marshall, one of the truly great Americans of the 20th century, is not as well known as he should be. This is undoubtedly because his name cannot be attached to any single wartime exploit (the Marshall Plan, for which he is best remembered, occurred after World War II). However, Marshall had the uncanny ability to recognize leadership potential. He was the person, as chief of staff and military adviser to the president, who selected all the top commanders of the Second World War: Eisenhower, Patton, MacArthur, people who became more famous than he. President Truman once said that he never rested comfortably as long as George Marshall was out of the country.

The ability to recognize leadership, which George Marshall possessed more than any other American, is probably more important than leadership itself. In the interest of fairness, or at least in the interest of being perceived as fair, corporations promote people into supervisory positions on the basis of objective performance standards, such as: education, years of service, job performance, attendance, etc. However, this is precisely the reason there are so many bad or mediocre managers in business today, especially at the lower echelons, where all of the work gets done. Perhaps the whole system has been designed, consciously or unconsciously, to select managers who don't rock the boat, who carry out the wishes of their superiors without comment or question, who follow the management guidebook and not common sense.

In the movie *The Train,* Paul Scofield plays a cultured Nazi colonel who's obsessed with the idea of transporting the best paintings in the Louvre museum to Germany, just as the Allies are preparing to liberate Paris. The only problem is that all the available trains are being used to move military supplies and he will need special permission from the German high command to release a train he has previously requisitioned for that purpose. In desperation, he bursts in on the general (writing some information on an easel, with his back to the door) who's in charge of allocating the trains:

General: [Turning momentarily to the colonel] What is it, Colonel?

Colonel: A train I ordered was cancelled. I've been advised your personal authorization is now required.

General: You can make application through normal channels.

Colonel: You once said normal channels were a trap in which to snare officers who lacked initiative.

General: [Abruptly turning to face the colonel] What's your cargo?

Over the years, in my experience in education, industry, the military, and sports, I've encountered some outstanding leaders. This has prompted me to analyze the reason(s) for their effectiveness. To my surprise, it turns out that good leaders comprise a variety of personality types. Some are talkative, some are not. Some are dynamic, some are shy. Some prefer to issue orders, others lead by example. However, they all seem to have some things in common. Here is my short list:

- Un-self-consciousness
  Good leaders don't analyze themselves or second-guess themselves. This does not mean that they can't accept suggestions or criticism. It simply means that after considering all the facts and making a decision, they don't worry about it. Harry Truman said he slept soundly the night after authorizing the use of the atomic bomb on Hiroshima and Nagasaki. Not that he

was insensitive to the appalling death and destruction which followed. But he had made the heart-wrenching calculation that many more people would have died otherwise, a large number of them American soldiers and marines, and that his first duty as Commander-in-Chief was to safeguard the lives of his troops.

- Authenticity
Good leaders don't try to be anything other than themselves. One of the things I despise about these management seminars or self-improvement courses is that they're phony. Or, more accurately, that they ask people to become something they're not. This the trouble with so much of our culture today: the fact that everything, including ourselves, is presented in a false light. Everything and everybody is beautiful, everyone is always smiling, everybody has our best interest at heart. This misrepresenting of reality has so permeated our consciousness that the result is naïvete on one hand or cynicism on the other. We have become so used to the idea of our leaders, whether in government, corporations, or even academia, not telling the truth that we're inclined not to believe anything they say. We *assume* that they're lying, prevaricating, or not giving us the whole story. What is so terrible about the truth? I've always thought that knowing the truth, no matter how distasteful, is better than uncertainty.

- Detachment
Good leaders don't need to be leaders. They'd be just as happy off by themselves in the woods somewhere,

118

taking a walk or felling a tree. During the Clinton Administration, I got the strong impression that Bill Clinton *needed* to be president, that being president was essential to his self-validation. At the end of his eight years in office, he did not go gently into that good night. The same thing was true, to a certain extent, of Nixon, Johnson, and Kennedy. It's interesting that this did not seem to be true of Ford and Truman, two of our *accidental* presidents (Johnson, though he was also *accidental*, had long wanted to be president). A certain reluctance on the part of a leader to be in charge has always been appealing. Think of Julius Caesar's twice refusing the "crown" before accepting it, knowing that his seeming detachment would endear him to the crowd.

- Sound Judgment
  Good leaders have the uncanny ability to distinguish between what is important and what is not. They can look at a complex situation, involving a multiplicity of options, and select the best course. Or, at a critical moment, they instinctively do the right thing. Perhaps one reason why someone does not make the correct decision at a time of crisis is that he/she gets bogged down in extraneous considerations, such as political correctness. The great leader doesn't worry about what the critics will say. This does not mean that the good leader is insensitive or lacks moral values. Indeed, this is already factored into any decision. A perfect example of a leader's ability to cut right to the heart of a crisis is FDR's First Inaugural Address, when he said: "The only thing we have to fear

is—fear itself!" He knew that the biggest problem America faced at the depths of the Great Depression was a loss of confidence. The people wanted to be told that someone was in charge and that everything would be all right. The flurry of activity that Roosevelt unleashed during the first 100 days of his presidency, though ultimately illusory and ineffective, convinced America that here was a man who understood their plight and would try anything to help them. This gave people the courage to confront their difficulties and ultimately triumph over them.

I realized early in life that I was temperamentally unsuited for any kind of leadership role. As the reader will undoubtedly surmise, I am introspective and self-conscious by nature, which according to my own criteria would disqualify me. But, in addition to that, I have a powerful aversion to telling the unadorned truth. Consequently, I have never made an attempt to secure a management position.

Fame

Fame is the reason people become movie stars and sports heroes. Of course, other motivations are present, too, such as "love of the game" and financial rewards. But the drive for fame is symptomatic of the basic human desire to "be somebody" or "make a difference." As Thoreau famously said, "The mass of men lead lives of quiet desperation." Fame presents a way out of this existential morass by convincing us that we are important, necessary people.

I've had three brief encounters with fame, all in high

school; and I must admit they were heady experiences. The first occurred during my junior year when I ran for student council president. As I recall, two or three candidates were selected from each homeroom. To my surprise (and delight, I must confess), I was one of them. I had never participated in student government before, and I really wasn't interested. However, I had made a number of friends in my first two and a half years and many more acquaintances. Although I gravitated toward the "intellectuals" in my class, I found that I had the ability to mix comfortably with all the various groups, such as the jocks, the hoods, and the "socials" (party people, actors, and other "cool" types). Without realizing it, I was developing the persona I would use for the rest of my life when dealing with people. Simply put, this consisted of deflecting attention away from myself by focusing on the other person. I accomplished this by first asking questions and then directing the conversation based on the answers to those questions. This did not mean that I lacked an ego. On the contrary, I was excessively self-absorbed. I craved attention, but I wanted to avoid the appearance of needing it or asking for it. Perhaps if I showed attention to others, they would reciprocate . . . ?

To return to the student council election: the next step was to take the list of nominees from the homerooms, about twenty-one students, and present them to the junior class as a whole. The top eight vote getters would then be considered as the final candidates in the general student council election, in which all the classes, except the seniors, would vote. This process would produce four officers: president, vice-president, secretary, and treasurer. The number of votes would determine which candidates would fill which offices: highest total would get the presidency, next highest the vice-presidency, etc. To my astonishment, I was among the final eight candidates.

The campaign could now begin. This meant that posters could be placed throughout the school. In this respect, I was unusually fortunate. In the junior class, consisting of about 200 students, there were four who were considered to have exceptional artistic talent. One of them, John Hanna, had been my locker mate for the last two years. Although we weren't close friends, we got along very well. John, who reminded me of the old-time movie actor Sterling Holloway, had a delightful sense of humor, which expressed itself most eloquently in his cartoons, which were often caricatures of our teachers or fellow students. John was a shy, gentle, retiring sort of person who portrayed the quirky, vulnerable side of his subjects without any trace of nastiness. He was the first to offer his services to me.

My next offer came from the second of the four premier artists, Joe Baczsko, a Hungarian émigré whose family came to the United States shortly after the failed uprising of 1956. In many ways, Joe was the antithesis of John. This became evident in Russian class, where Joe had an ongoing confrontation with the teacher, Alexei Tsurikov, whose family had emigrated from Russia after the Revolution. Even though Mr. Tsurikov was anything but a Communist, I think Joe resented the fact that he was Russian, since it was the Russians who ultimately put down the Hungarian rebellion, and brutally at that. Once, after a nasty verbal exchange, it seemed that Joe and Mr. Tsurikov might come to blows. It was Joe who created the most memorable—and controversial—poster of the campaign: a voluptuous woman, obviously a prostitute, leaning seductively against a lamppost.

The caption read: "Get in shape with H—!" The administration were not amused. After a day or two, they demanded that the poster be removed. I took it home, where I kept it (hidden) for a long time afterward.

My final offer came from Jim Connor, brilliant underachiever and third of the four artist superstars. In addition to what was reported to be a genius IQ, Jim had a caustic wit, which was reflected in his art. His older brother John had preceded him at McQuaid and was now in his first year at Fordham, where I would eventually go myself. John had excelled both academically and in extracurriculars, notably debating. As so often happens, great things are expected of the subsequent siblings, and comparisons, though odious, are inevitably made. I suspected that Jim rebelled against those expectations. His academic record was good, but everybody thought it should have been a lot better. Jim didn't seem to care, though. I think he got a perverse pleasure out of disappointing his teachers.

With all that high-powered artistic talent working for me, I should have won the election; but I didn't even finish in the top four.

The posters, however, were at best a side show. The real culmination of the campaign, which lasted about three weeks, was the speeches: each candidate would address the entire assembled student body, excluding the seniors. This was the part that scared me. Actually, there was only one of us who wasn't scared: Ferdinand J. Smith, who had achieved fame as an orator and debater since freshman year and who would later, as head of his own advertising agency, become the top voice-over man in our area. The rest of us were amateurs by comparison.

I had never spoken before a large group, and I was naturally apprehensive. In fact, when the final eight candidates were first announced, I was tempted to withdraw my name. But the lure of fame was too strong. As the day of the speeches approached, I worked on mine. It was full of the usual platitudes about honesty, integrity, etc. I showed it to a couple of trusted classmates whose opinion I valued. I was particularly gratified and heartened when one of them, Tom Sable, who was respected for his frank criticism, gave me his endorsement. However, I realized that it was the delivery, more than the speech itself, which was going to be decisive in getting people's votes.

My speech was short, only about four to five minutes. After committing it to memory, I worked on my presentation. I wanted to be dignified without being wooden. I wanted my voice to be strong and clear, but not forced. I wanted to be assured and confident without being arrogant. And, of course, I didn't want to stumble over any of my words.

As I approached the podium on that Friday afternoon, I struggled to keep calm. I started slowly, reciting the standard greeting: "Father Principal, most honored faculty, fellow students . . ." The first two or three sentences were just slightly tentative, but not noticeable to anyone but myself. There were no mistakes, so I decided to pick up the pace a bit. After a minute or so, with things proceeding smoothly, I began to relax a little. Then, about two minutes into my speech, I actually started to enjoy myself. I panned the audience, pausing momentarily to check the expression on someone's face, then moving on. They were paying attention! By the end, I was hooked. I almost wished I had more to say.

With the exception of Ferdinand J. Smith, the "professional" orator, I thought I had done as well as anyone else that day. In the final analysis, however, despite a good speech and the best campaign posters, I didn't have as good a name recognition as my opponents. They had all played varsity sports (football and/or basketball) or had otherwise distinguished themselves in extracurricular activities, such as acting, newspaper writing, or student council. I didn't finish "in the money." And so my brief political career came to an end.

My second brush with fame occurred in late winter of my senior year. This time it was acting which gave me my chance.

As part of Senior Weekend, the organizers wanted to put on a play. There were several fine actors in the senior class, but the idea was to give other people a chance, people who had never acted before. My Greek teacher, Jim Bowes, volunteered his class to stage a production of Aeschylus' *Choephori* (*The Libation Bearers*), second play in the Oresteia trilogy. This was a classic example of "killing two birds with one stone." Mr. Bowes wanted to teach us about Greek tragedy by allowing us to perform one. Originally, the play was to be done only in class, with the students functioning as both actors and observers. There were more students than parts (excluding the chorus), so Mr. Bowes came up with the idea of doing the play with several teams of actors, each of which would do a part of the play. When one team was performing, the rest would comprise the chorus.

Some of us in Greek class were also in Ed Zogby's English class. Ed was also moderator of the Dramatics Club. When he heard that we were doing a Greek tragedy, he immediately realized the comic possibilities of having different actors playing the same parts. He asked Jim if he could adapt

The Libation Bearers for Senior Weekend. Thus was Aeschylus' noble tragedy commuted to comedy.

To prevent the audience (which consisted of the senior class and their dates) from becoming hopelessly confused by a succession of different actors playing Orestes, Agamemnon, etc., someone came up with the idea of color-coding the tunics. In other words, the actors playing Orestes (of whom I was one) would all wear green, those playing Agamemnon would all wear white, etc. As a result, a lot of old bed sheets were dyed and converted into tunics by cutting holes for the head and arms. A final touch was added by using a piece of old clothesline or sash cord for a belt.

Our natural ineptitude as actors, the succession of actors playing the same parts, and some fortuitous onstage blunders combined to produce a memorable evening, which both we and the audience thoroughly enjoyed. The high point for me, of course, came when it was my turn to play Orestes. I had a few short lines, followed by a fairly long speech. I wasn't afraid of botching my lines or anything, since by that point in the play (I was the third and next-to-last Orestes) copious mistakes had been made, all to the delight of the performers as well as the audience. A large part of the humor stemmed from the contrast in acting styles and abilities, as each different actor assumed the same role. A few actors tried to be funny, but most of us tried to play it straight, allowing the humor to come from blown lines, stilted delivery, or both. Once again, as during my campaign speech the previous year, I was exhilarated by the experience of standing before a large audience, knowing that everyone's attention was focused on *me*. But this was even more thrilling, because that audience included scores of girls, one of whom was my date, a particularly enchanting young lady whom I was in love with and wanted to impress. My initial nervousness overcome, I began to relax about two-thirds of the way through my speech and even hammed it up a bit. At that moment I understood the lure of the stage. But this was to be my first and last performance.

My final taste of fame occurred a few months later at the graduation ceremony, which took place on a Saturday evening at the prestigious Eastman Theater, a showcase for the best in music, built for the city of Rochester by George Eastman himself. A large number of my family were there, including most of my aunts, uncles, and cousins from both sides. My girlfriend Betsy was there, too, sitting with my immediate family. I wasn't expecting anything unusual that night. I, along with 162 of my classmates, would walk down the aisle when my name was called and receive my diploma from the guest of honor, Bishop Kearney. Following this would be the presentation of the valedictorian and salutatorian awards, the accompanying speeches, and then the closing address by the Bishop. At least, that's what was on the published program.

After the salutatory speech, however, there occurred one of those truly landmark events in life, where surprise meshes perfectly with joy. The principal, Fr. Cornelius Carr, stepped to the podium and, instead of introducing the Bishop as expected, proceeded to mention something about another award, the Bishop Kearney Award, so named in honor of the man sitting in the chair of honor. The award, which hadn't been given since 1959 (four years ago), was to be presented to the student who in the eyes of the faculty best represented the ideals of the school; in other words, the "Ideal McQuaid Student." He added that it was the highest award the school could bestow.

Then he read the name inscribed on the face plate: *Mine*!

In the words of Andy Warhol, I had achieved my fifteen minutes of fame. From that point on, it was all downhill. I guess you could say that I had peaked too early.

Romance

Of the four arenas of success listed at the beginning of this chapter, romance is the only one I was ever seriously interested in. And it was my second choice at that.

As related earlier, my first serious career thoughts were of the priesthood. I probably would have been ordained, too, had it not been for Betsy, the girl who invited me to a dance in the fall of 1962, just after I had made up my mind to apply for admission to the Jesuits.

In retrospect, my acceptance of Betsy's invitation changed the course of my life. If I had said no, as I was inclined to do, that would have been the end of my social life, especially if word had gotten out that I was considering the priesthood. In those days, any boy headed for the priesthood was considered untouchable, even unapproachable. But for some inexplicable reason, I accepted Betsy's invitation. It wasn't that I was afraid to say no. I had refused at least one other invitation the previous year. And it wasn't that I thought Betsy was particularly attractive, either. I had seen her only a few times: at baseball games, when she babysat my coach's little boy, and in church, where she attended daily Mass. We had never spoken to each other prior to the night she called and asked me to the dance. She hadn't made any impression on me—at least as compared to some other girls I had seen on the bus. The only thing I can think of that made me accept was the opportunity it presented to gain some social exposure prior to being locked up in a seminary, where there would be no contact with the opposite sex.

My experience of women before Betsy was limited to movies, television, and family. From the beginning, I was fascinated by the way women *looked*: not by their physical attributes, such as breasts, but by their clothes, particularly the high, stiletto heels that were coming into fashion in the late 1950s. Of course, they had to have pretty faces, too.

There were two particularly cute girls that I'd see on the bus every day. One of my favorite pastimes was to imagine what they would look like fully decked out in their feminine attire. School didn't offer any opportunities for the girls to dress up. Everyone wore the same drab uniform. In fact, the idea was to make the girls look as homely as possible, so that the boys wouldn't get any ideas.

But dances were another matter. The girls could dress any way they wanted, within reason. And so it was that when Betsy and her parents picked me up that evening for the dance, I was totally devastated. All my plans—all my thoughts—were instantly and irrevocably changed. The orderly, priestly life I had envisioned for myself suddenly didn't mean anything any more. From the moment she stepped out of the car, and I saw her resplendent in blue dress, nylon stockings, and high heels, all I could think about was Betsy.

In many ways, my reaction was normal. I felt myself getting physically aroused. I was alarmed and ashamed, and I tried to hide it. Due to my naïvete about such matters, I didn't realize that there was nothing unusual about this. If I had been to dances before, I probably wouldn't have reacted so strongly. Years later, when I reflected on this, I realized that it was the *appearance* of women that excited me, not the anticipation or the actual experience of lovemaking.

Unbeknownst to me, I was confusing the preliminaries with the main event. This was to have a profound and devastating effect on all my subsequent attempts to find romance.

However, despite my enchantment with Betsy's appearance, it would be wrong to say that that's all there was to my fascination with her. From that moment on, I was in love with her. I was thrilled every time I saw her or spoke to her, even in the mundane surroundings of the bus ride home.

I was heavily involved with the school newspaper then. One day, after working on the paper, I happened to meet Betsy downtown. She evidently was involved in some extracurricular activity of her own; and since we both lived in the same area, we had to take the same bus home. (This was not the school bus, but the city bus. In order to get home after extracurriculars, we both had to take a city bus downtown and then transfer to another city bus.) Anyway, after that first accidental meeting, I tried to arrange my after-school schedule so as to provide the best chance of seeing her downtown. I found myself staying after school even when there was nothing to do at the newspaper office. On average, I probably managed to see her once a week. What's that line from *The King and I* ("Hello, Young Lovers"):

You fly down the street on the chance that you'll meet
But you meet not really by chance.

Without repeating a story that has been told elsewhere (Chapter 2), my romance with Betsy ultimately failed. But so did my association with the Jesuits, which was the ostensible reason for my failure with Betsy. Actually, the Jesuits and

Betsy were inextricably connected: each caused the other to fail.

In terms of a career, the Jesuit priesthood was the only thing I've ever seriously considered. In subsequent years, I thought about trying to go back. But each time I got close to making up my mind, it was the thought of a possible romance that prevented me from reapplying. Ironically, when I eventually gave up the idea of reentering the Jesuits, it wasn't because of romance. It was due to the philosophical and behavioral conflicts that would have inevitably ensued.

During my sophomore year in college, when I realized that both Betsy and the Jesuits were definitively over (at least for the foreseeable future), I began to look for something to replace what I had lost. This became the quest for The Ideal Woman. Little did I know that it was hopeless from the start. Romance, like the more general condition happiness, cannot be approached directly. It just *happens*—and usually when you least expect it. As a result of this and other experiences, I've adopted the following rule of life:

Nothing succeeds like indifference.[1]

Or, as Harry Truman used to say, the only way a bank

---

[1] "Detachment" is a better word. "Indifference" implies that one doesn't care how things turn out. "Detachment," on the other hand, does not imply that one doesn't care; it simply means that one accepts the outcome of uncontrollable events with equanimity. However, I used "indifference" in the quote above for three reasons: (1) The person whom I originally heard it from used that word. (2) As a strategy in the game of love, which is the context of the original quote, it is more apropos. (3) "Indifference" sounds better and is more easily understood.

131

will lend you money is to prove to them that you don't need it.

An Alternative Definition of Success

There may be ways of achieving success other than those discussed above. For myself, I've abandoned any hope or desire of earthly success. Instinctively, I've always known that it would be futile for me to pursue the normal paths to fulfillment. Even a life based on the idea of helping others, which had such a strong appeal to me in adolescence, no longer makes sense to me—*as a career.* The kind of help people want is usually directed toward the accomplishment of one or more kinds of earthly success, such as the four types discussed in this chapter, something which I have rejected on philosophical and experiential grounds as being unworthy of serious consideration. The only way I would make a career out of helping others is if I were convinced I possessed the secret of the meaning of life; in which case, I would feel compelled to share this knowledge with everyone.

On the other hand, *as a human being,* I have an obligation to help anyone I come in contact with, regardless of what type of need that person has.

I would like to venture an alternative definition of success, which is finding the answers to the two questions posed at the beginning of this book:

1. What is the meaning of life in general?
2. What is the meaning of *my* life?

7. Ethics

Priest:	Do you know what Our Lord said to the woman taken in adultery?
Lara:	Yes, father. He said go and sin no more.
Priest:	And did she?
Lara:	I don't know, father.
Priest:	Nobody does, child. Flesh is not weak. It is *strong*. And the sacrament of marriage will contain it. Remember that.

—Doctor Zhivago

Overview

In his excellent book *Slouching Towards Gomorrah,*[1] subtitled *Modern Liberalism and American Decline,* Robert Bork discusses the factors contributing to what he considers the deterioration of American culture. Chief among these is the weakening of the churches, which he believes has caused the disintegration of the moral values essential to the health of a society. In other words, Bork sees a direct link between religion and morality.

---

[1] Robert H. Bork, *Slouching Towards Gomorrah: Modern Liberalism and American Decline* (New York, HarperCollins, 1996).

To be precise, it is the mainline Christian Churches which are the subject of his analysis, as opposed to the Evangelical Christian Churches, which are thriving. Among the mainline Christian Churches Bork includes the traditional Protestant denominations, such as the Baptists, Methodists, Lutherans, and Presbyterians, as well as the Episcopal Church and the Roman Catholic Church. Prior to the 1960s, these organizations accounted for the vast majority of churchgoers in the United States. These churches were in general agreement on most theological and moral issues; and, for the most part, they were uncompromising in their positions.

Bork argues that since the 1960s, these churches have softened their views on some of these issues and/or have allowed their members greater latitude in thought and action. The result has been a slow but steady undermining of the moral code and a gradual weakening of the churches' authority in faith and morals. In other words, "everybody does their own thing."

During this same time, Bork notes a decline in membership in the mainline churches; whereas, in the evangelical churches, membership has been increasing. He asks whether this is due to the fact that the mainline churches are not requiring enough of their members. The evangelicals, on the other hand, make strict doctrinal and ethical demands on their members.

I accept Bork's analysis as far as it goes. As one who grew up a Roman Catholic in the 1950s, I can attest to the rigor and clarity of the Church's moral and theological pronouncements. These were promulgated from the pulpit on Sunday, in the classroom from Monday though Friday, and any time there was an adult in my presence. My indoctrination was so complete and so thorough that I think I was almost psychologically incapable of committing an immoral act. Moreover, I was afraid to go anywhere or do anything which might put me in a compromising situation (i.e., I avoided "the *occasions* of sin").

Things began to change in the 1960s. With the accession of Pope John XXIII in 1959 and his convening of the Second Vatican Council, the Church underwent a prolonged period of self-examination and reflection. This caused intense excitement within the Church. It was as if all the windows of the stuffy old structure were flung open and a torrent of fresh air came rushing through, clearing out the dust of centuries. I myself was caught up in the ferment, deciding in the fall of 1962 to enter the Society of Jesus. After I left the Jesuits to attend college, the effects of Vatican II were beginning to be felt in the classroom. Situation Ethics was the hot new thing. Instead of solving an ethical crisis by rote adherence to Canon Law, we were given the option of applying situational guidelines. In other words, an action which formerly might have been prohibited by unqualified reference to the Ten Commandments might be permitted under certain circumstances. For example: lying, which is forbidden by the Eighth Commandment, could be justified to save a person's life.

Gradually I, along with the rest of society, began to apply the principles of Situation Ethics more and more liberally until eventually I stopped applying them altogether. I did pretty much whatever I wanted. In reality, however, there was only one area where my conduct was in conflict with the Catholic Church's teaching: sex. I didn't lie, I didn't steal (unless you want to include cheating on my income tax), I didn't mistreat anyone. And, for the most part, I believe society behaved the same way.

In other words, there is a wide range of human conduct in which it is possible to do the right thing comfortably, without any serious challenge to one's normal, habitual behavior patterns. Indeed, society is increasingly set up this way, so that people can go about their lives without ever feeling guilty about anything. A lot of this is due to the influence of the mass media, particularly in the area of advertising, where people are continuously encouraged to indulge themselves by all manner of means. They are absolved of guilt by the assertion that life is getting tougher and tougher and therefore they are entitled to a reward. It's not inconceivable that we will eventually get to a point where we spend our entire lives in pursuit of compensation for having done nothing.

Occasionally, however, one may be presented with a situation involving a stark moral choice, from which there is, in Sartre's memorable phrase, "*No Exit.*" This happened to me in 1980 when I got a woman whom I'd been dating pregnant. Suddenly, I found myself in a moral no man's land, where all my upbringing and education were useless. However, the reality was that ever since I had left the Jesuits in 1963, the ethical dimension of my life was in steady decline, so that by 1980 there was very little moral sensitivity left. But there was just enough to cause a profound sense of guilt and revulsion[2] when my girl friend decided to have an abortion, an act which I had always felt was an abomination, but which now seemed

---

[2] I later confessed my involvement to a priest.

136

the only sensible thing to do. The traditional religious response to an "accidental" pregnancy was for the mother to have the baby and then put it up for adoption, if it proved impracticable for her to raise the child herself. This is the course of action I would have favored had I not been personally involved. (That changes everything, doesn't it? Morality is no longer an exercise in applying abstract rules to other people's lives. You look at things a lot differently when it's *your* life on the line.) There was also the option of a "shotgun wedding," which I had witnessed firsthand when one of my adolescent friends got his girl friend pregnant in 1963. This turned out to be a disaster, as most such marriages are, which is probably why this solution is not as popular now as it was in the past.

In short, we've gone from a morality of strict adherence to rules to a morality of live and let live, where you can do whatever you want as long as nobody gets hurt.[3]

The Connection Between Religion and Morality

I believe Robert Bork is correct when he states that the decline in moral standards is directly attributable to the decline in religion. By religion, he means membership in a church, regular attendance and support, and loyalty to its precepts. The decline is due to the fact that most people don't take their religion seriously any more. The Christian churches (evangelicals and fundamentalists excepted) don't

---

[3] This, of course, depends on one's idea of what is hurtful, which obviously will vary widely from person to person.

take themselves seriously either, as evidenced by their un-willingness to make strict demands on their members.

The reasons for the churches' decline are complicated, but it boils down to this: the churches have become businesses. As such, they depend on their "customers." To keep your customers and attract new ones, you need to have an attractive product. You need to be "relevant." The traditional messages of self-control, self-restraint, and self-sacrifice do not seem to resonate in today's hedonistic culture, where self-indulgence is supreme. Hence, organized mainstream religion, in an attempt to harmonize with the times and remain solvent, has scaled back its moral and theological content to the point of meaninglessness. So people naturally ask: why bother?

Historically, religions have always contained an explicit or implicit moral code. This code comes directly from the founder (or God Himself), as in the Ten Commandments; or it may be the logical consequence of the religion's underlying principles, as in the Catholic Church's teaching on abortion. Since religious experience by nature is not subject to the same methods of inquiry and verification as in science and mathematics, religion's credibility has suffered over the preceding five centuries. In contemporary America, it has been relegated to the realm of superstition by the intelligentsia and the mainstream media. It is almost impossible nowadays to have a serious, intellectual discussion concerning religion. No wonder that the embedded ethical teachings of religion are discredited as well.

The major problem with morality, as it relates to religion, is that it is generally presented as a package deal which one must accept or reject. In other words, adherence to the moral code is purely and simply an *act of will*. This is the reason why the Catholic Church has traditionally placed so much emphasis on maintaining its own school system, in spite of the financial burden imposed on its members, who for the most part have been only too happy to bear it, confident that the moral education of their children would be secure. However, children who are brought up under this system tend to obey the Church's moral code blindly, with little or no consideration of its theological or philosophical underpinnings. This is precisely the intent: to forestall any questioning or doubt. In the Church's view, morality is something which must be learned and practiced by rote, so that it becomes automatic. It's like a soldier in basic training. The discipline is designed to make him obey orders instantly and without question.

This approach to morality has proven very effective over the centuries. The Church's attitude was: what difference does it make whether a person understands the reasons for acting a certain way, as long as he does the right thing? Of course, blind obedience to religious authority can have disastrous consequences, as we have seen in our own day.

The problem with this approach to ethics is that everything depends on the conditioning, which over time can be eroded by continued exposure to contrary ideas, as from the entertainment and advertising media. Educated and intellectually curious people are particularly vulnerable, because they tend to analyze and question things (such as a moral code that they learned as children). It's pretty difficult to retain a strong sense of personal self-restraint, required for adherence to a strict moral code, when subjected to a constant barrage of messages that justify and encourage self-indulgence. Most people today, when presented with an opportunity for potentially harmful pleasure (be it sex, drink, drugs, etc.), would find it impossible to resist. Indeed, so powerful and pervasive is the current culture of self-gratification that they would probably have no doubt or hesitation in "seizing the moment." Such is what preoccupied me from the 70s through the 90s.

It would seem that unaided[4] will, therefore, is insufficient to sustain a moral code.

Situation Ethics attempted to allow the individual some degree of latitude in interpreting the moral code in light of specific circumstances. However, this often degenerated into mere rationalization. If one was ingenious and determined enough, almost any action could be justified.

An alternative approach to Situation Ethics is the idea that a moral code can be established on a philosophical basis so compelling that non-compliance is practically impossible. This has appeared in many guises and under many names:

- "Virtue is knowledge"
- Kant's categorical imperative
- The Golden Rule
- Enlightened self-interest

The idea underlying all of these is that people would act morally if they fully understood the consequences of *not* acting morally; for example, the damage that might result from

---

[4] Orthodox Christian teaching has always asserted that man, left to his own devices (i.e., without God's grace), is incapable of "justification," which is living in such a way as to be worthy of entering the Kingdom of God.

an action or the sorrow it might cause other people, including oneself. In the realm of actual experience (as opposed to theory), this idea can work powerfully to change a person's behavior. For example, suppose a person has a drinking problem. Typically, such a person is in denial. But suppose this person, as a direct result of his drinking, is involved in a car crash that kills another person. Such an event could be so traumatic and literally sobering that the person who caused the accident might never take another drink. A similar change in behavior could result from an extramarital affair, in which the unsuspecting wife or husband might be driven to murder or suicide, causing the offenders to take a different view of infidelity.

Of course, the above approach and examples deal mainly with the proscriptive side of morality: things that *shouldn't* be done (cf. the Ten Commandments). Determining what *should* be done is a different (and much more difficult) proposition and is a recurring theme of this book.

Theoretically, the above approach to morality sounds like it should work; and for certain people, I believe it has. Socrates, for example, or Marcus Aurelius. The problem is that the average person, not philosophically inclined, might find the reasoning process too complicated or abstract. Besides, this approach is based not so much on religion as on philosophy; and it is the connection between religion and morality that we are examining.

An Alternative View of Religion and Morality

I would like to propose another way of examining the connection between religion and morality, specifically from the standpoint of Christianity. My starting point is Chapter 12 of the Gospel of Saint Mark:

And one of the Scribes came forward . . . and . . . asked him which was the first commandment of all. But Jesus answered him, "The first commandment of all is, 'Hear, O Israel! The Lord our God is one God; and thou shalt love the Lord thy God with thy whole heart, and with thy whole soul, and with thy whole mind, and with thy whole strength.' This is the first commandment. And the second is like it, 'Thou shalt love thy neighbor as thyself.' There is no other commandment greater than these."[5]

The above passage contains the entire moral code of Christianity. The Ten Commandments, which are mainly *pro*scriptive ("don't do this, don't do that"), have been reduced to two, both of them *pre*scriptive. This fact by itself is significant. But more about this in due course. For now, I would like to focus first on the meaning of the two commandments, then on their logical connection.

The literal meaning of the first commandment seems straightforward enough: we're supposed to love God to the greatest degree possible. Okay. But how can we love God without knowing Him? As human beings, it is impossible for us to love someone without at least being acquainted with him. So how do we get to know God?

As with any relationship, there are two[6] possibilities: ei-

---

[5] Mark 12:28–31.

[6] I suppose a third possibility is an *accidental* encounter or association, in which people are brought together by chance, as at a party or at work. But where God is concerned, I wonder if anything is really accidental.

ther God approaches us or we approach God. The first possibility is obviously out of our control. We don't know if or when God will approach us. It's exactly like the relationship I had with Betsy, my first girlfriend. She approached me completely out of the blue. If she hadn't called and asked me to a dance, I would never have known her. But that serendipitous event changed the course of my life.

The second possibility, our approaching God, *is* in our control; but it's not something which is done casually, like taking a walk or stopping for a beer. The decision to seek God is usually the result of an event or condition in our lives which causes us to reject, or at least to question, the things that we normally seek, such as wealth, power, love, etc. Based on my observations, I would say that most people achieve enough satisfaction out of these things, so that they don't feel the need for anything deeper. However, as Saint Augustine points out, man is essentially a spiritual being who cannot be truly satisfied by anything but God.

And so man approaches God out of spiritual hunger, realizing that nothing material can satisfy him. The circumstances which force a person to this realization are as varied as people themselves. For example, in Somerset Maugham's novel *The Razor's Edge,* the hero returns home after the First World War in a state of disillusionment. A close friend died; he didn't. It could just as easily have been the other way around. Why? His fiancée, his family, and his friends expect him to resume the life he had led before the war. But he realizes that that is impossible. He has seen too much and thought too much. He is frustrated because he can't make them understand. And so, forsaking his sweetheart and a conventional life, he embarks on a spiritual quest, culminating in the

Himalayan Mountains of India, where a holy man facilitates his encounter with God.

Following this encounter, the hero is transformed. He can never look at life the same way again. He achieves a kind of transcendence, a detachment from worldly concerns. He is *in* the world but not *of* it.

A transformative event is irreversible; i.e., it prevents you from looking at things the way you did before the event occurred. Something like this must have happened when Galileo first turned his telescope on the heavens. What he saw changed his understanding of the world forever. No longer was it possible to regard the Earth as the center of the universe.

The moral consequences of an encounter with God are similarly transformative and irreversible. This is why Jesus Christ was unable to commit sin: He was, by definition (i.e., as God's "son"), continually in the presence of God. If sin is defined as anything which separates us from God,[7] then anyone who is in touch with God cannot sin. This, in a nutshell, is the connection between religion and morality.

Let's return now to the quotation from Saint Mark, where the commandment to love God is placed before the commandment to love one another. Logically, the reason why love of God precedes love of neighbor (which could be extended to include all of God's creation) is that loving God

---

[7] This is what happened to Adam and Eve in the Garden of Eden. The Bible tells us that Adam and Eve, while in the Garden, were in constant communication with God. Sin, which occurred when Adam and Eve ate the Forbidden Fruit, caused them to be expelled from the Garden, resulting in their separation from God, which is the condition man has been in ever since.

makes it possible to love our neighbor. We are able to love our neighbor as God does; i.e., without qualification or without limit. Such love makes a proscriptive moral code unnecessary. Instead of worrying about the things we shouldn't do, we become preoccupied with finding ways to enhance the being of all around us.

Note the sequence of events:

- We encounter God.
- We know God.
- We love God ("to know Him is to love Him").
- We love our neighbor (which by extension includes all of God's creation, the manifestation of God in time).

This goes far beyond morality. It is, in reality, the way to holiness.

8. Politics

Conover:	You may as well sit in here and be comfortable. I have a radio . . . Dare I listen?
Kay:	You can listen.
Conover:	Are you sure? You were only with him a few minutes.
Kay:	And Mary's had weeks. I know. It wasn't hard, Jim. All I did was to tell him the things he wanted to hear. But there is one question on his mind you'd better have the answer for.
Conover:	What's that?
Kay:	He's beginning to wonder if there is any difference between the Democratic Party and the Republican Party.
Conover:	Now that's a fine question for a presidential candidate to ask. There's all the difference in the world. They're in and we're out.

—*State of the Union*

Overview

If ethics is the philosophy of individual behavior, as it relates to the moral conduct of one's life, then politics may be defined as the philosophy of collective behavior. In other words, politics deals with the question of how large groups of

146

people, organized as nations, are to get along among themselves (i.e., domestic affairs) and with each other (i.e., foreign relations).

In the chapter on ethics, I tried to explore the connection between religion and morality: to show how man's relationship with God is crucial to his ability to live a moral life and thereby achieve his destiny, which is union with God. Is there a similar connection between religion and politics? Or, to put the question another way, is there a collective destiny for man? Does God care how man organizes himself politically?

Perhaps an answer to this fundamental question can be achieved by exploring a series of other questions, such as:

- How does politics impinge on an individual's life; e.g., does politics affect man's ability to live morally and find God?
- What can history tell us about the relationship of politics and the individual?
- Is one political system better than another?
- Is there such a thing as political evolution?

Politics and the Individual

Does politics affect man's ability to live morally and find God? The short answer is "Yes," but some explanation is required.

In order for man to act morally (or immorally, for that matter), he must be *free*. But freedom can mean many things. Maybe a better way of saying this is that freedom exists on different levels. For example, there is freedom of:

- Movement
- Choice
- Speech
- Thought

Freedom of movement is the most basic. It simply means that you are not confined or restrained. A person serving a prison sentence does not have this kind of freedom.

Freedom of choice means that you can do what you want. For example, you can go to the store or go to a movie. You can drive your car or you can walk. You can spend a romantic weekend at the beach or you can stay home alone. In most societies, however, there are limitations on what you can do. In some Muslim countries, for example, women cannot go outside without covering their faces. Committing an unlawful act usually results in some form of punishment.

Freedom of speech means that you can say what you want to in public (i.e., in the presence of other people). In America, freedom of speech has traditionally meant freedom of political expression. However, in recent times, this has been extended to other public forms of expression, such as pornography and prayer. There is now a heated debate over whether there should be any restrictions on this type of freedom.

Freedom of thought is simply the freedom to think whatever you want. At first glance, it would seem that there would be no way to control a person's thoughts. A person could theoretically be deprived of all his other freedoms and still be free in his own mind. In the movie *Dr. Zhivago*, for example, there is a scene in which Zhivago and his family are forced to share a boxcar with some political prisoners who are chained to their bunks. One of the prisoners, an intellectual with obvious disdain for the people around him, exclaims:

I'm the only free man on this train!

The sad fact is, however, that it *is* possible to control a person's thoughts. *The Manchurian Candidate* presents a chilling example of brainwashing, where an American prisoner of war is transformed into a killing machine by his captors. All that's required to "activate" him is a word or an image, such as the Queen of Diamonds on a playing card. In Nazi Germany, ordinary citizens were turned into cold-blooded executioners, who could murder hundreds, even thousands, of defenseless victims without compassion or remorse. In the Middle East, children are instructed in the ways of Islamic Fundamentalism so thoroughly that they grow up to become fanatical terrorists, intent on murdering themselves and everyone else. Less dramatic and destructive examples are visible all around us.

Freedom of thought is crucial for man's existence as man. A person without freedom of thought is not fully human. Any political system which deprives man of his freedom to think prevents him from acting morally.

Fundamentally, from the standpoint of human freedom, there are only two political systems: totalitarian and democratic. Examples of the former are the Roman Empire, the Soviet Union, and Afghanistan (under Taliban rule). Examples of the latter are ancient Athens, the Weimar Republic, and the United States. In totalitarian systems, power is concentrated in the hands of a few privileged people; in democratic systems, power is distributed among the ordinary citizens and/or their representatives. Totalitarian regimes try to control their subjects by restricting their freedoms. Modern totalitarian states have learned that the best way to accomplish this is by controlling people's thoughts. Democracies, on the other hand, permit the free exchange of ideas and information. This allows each individual citizen to make up his own mind about what to think and what to do.

A Historical Perspective

What does the historical record indicate in regard to the origin and development of political systems? Do we appear to be heading in any particular direction?

By nature, man is a social and therefore political animal. From the basic family unit of man, woman, and children there arose the tribe. Tribes banded together, probably for protection, into larger units until something like a nation-state emerged. Democracy appears to have originated in ancient Greece, most notably exemplified by Athens in the Fifth Century before Christ. There was also a democracy of sorts in pre-Empire Rome, where power was distributed at least among the Senators, if not the common people.

However, from the beginning of the Roman Empire under Julius Caesar (about 43 B.C.E.) until the 13th Century, democracy all but disappeared. The signing of the Magna Carta in 1215 was the first serious limitation on imperial power, paving the way for the gradual development of democracy in England, which spilled over into colonial America. The United

States, following its successful rebellion against English rule, was the first nation in the world to be *founded* as a democracy.[1] It has remained so ever since and is still evolving.

The United States, as the world's oldest continuous democratic nation, illustrates some of the problems inherent in a democratic society. Theoretically, one would think that democracy is the ideal form of government, at least in terms of its advantages for the individual citizen. Such a political system would seem to provide maximum freedom for the individual, which, as we noted above, is a prerequisite for him to act morally. However, as Alexis de Tocqueville first pointed out in his *Democracy in America,* written not long after the United States was born, there is a built-in conflict between freedom and equality, originating in the Declaration of Independence, which predates the Constitution. The Declaration states that all men are not only *free*; they are *equal.*[2] Herein lies the historical basis for the philosophical difference between America's two major political parties. The Republicans have traditionally stressed freedom; the Democrats, particularly since FDR, have stressed equality. This is why the Republicans typically oppose legislation which attempts to restrict the freedoms of individuals and corporations, arguing that such legislation stifles the energy

---

[1] Technically, the United States is a republic, in which the voice of the people is expressed indirectly through their elected representatives. In a true democracy, the people decide issues by direct vote, as in ancient Athens.

[2] The precise nature of this equality is the subject of a spirited debate. Its original meaning seems to have been *equality before the law.* Conservative Republican critics have charged that Democrats have extended this to mean *equality of outcomes.*

and creativity necessary to keep America competitive in the world. Democrats counter that such a philosophy favors the rich and powerful, leading to greater economic and social disparities among America's citizens.

Another aspect of democracy is its implicit faith in the collective wisdom of the marketplace, which assumes the free exchange of ideas as well as commodities. As long as everyone plays fairly, the best goods and ideas should prevail.

The historical record seems to bear this out—at least over the long haul. For example, in the later part of the 19th Century and early 20th, the monopolies and the trusts and the robber barons wielded tremendous power, not always to the advantage of American society. A sense of outrage developed among certain segments of the population, including the press. Eventually, a people's champion emerged in the person of Teddy Roosevelt, who led the fight to rein in corporate power and curb some of its more conspicuous excesses. Later, at the height of the Great Depression, when the American Dream had died for millions of Americans, another champion emerged, also named Roosevelt.

The point is that a democratic society such as America, despite a long history of injustice, inequality, and sheer folly, has the capacity to critique and ultimately correct itself.

Since America is a huge, complex, and increasingly diverse nation, it is difficult to achieve consensus on a number of issues, such as abortion, school prayer, and censorship. However—and this is the crucial point—there is still fundamental agreement on the rules of behavior for conducting public debate. Even though some political ideologues are becoming more strident, more doctrinaire, and more uncompromising, none of them would seriously suggest that their opponents be prevented from contributing their views. Democrats and Republicans don't battle each other for control of the streets, as did the Nazis and the Communists in the waning years of the Weimar Republic.

Political Evolution?

Is there an evolutionary trend in politics? Again, the short answer is "Yes"; and again, some explanation is required.

The trend in world politics is unquestionably toward democracy. The nations of Europe—including Russia[3]—are democratic. In the not-so-distant past, two of these countries were ruled by the most brutal totalitarian regimes in history. In Asia, the same could be said of Japan. India has emerged from colonial rule into a thriving democracy, while South Korea, formerly a province of Imperial Japan, is also democratic. International Communism, which during the mid-20th Century appeared to be in the ascendancy, is now in retreat. China, Cuba, and North Korea are the main remnants from this period, but major change may be waiting in the wings. China may become more democratic under capitalist market pressure, while Cuba awaits the death of Castro. North Korea, however, seems determined to remain in menacing isolation, at least for the foreseeable future.

A word of warning, though. In order to be successful,

---

[3] Russia is nominally democratic, but it may be some time before it is irreversibly so. Unfortunately, there are elements of Russian society which would favor a return to a totalitarian state.

democracy depends on two things: economic well-being (or at least a reasonable hope of such in the near future) and a liberal education. The major threat to democracy is currently coming from the Islamic world, where ignorance and deprivation are being parlayed into a fanatical hatred of Western Civilization. Some of the people behind this may be sincere, believing that the West is sinful and corrupt. Others may be mere demagogues. Either way, extremist Islam presents the greatest challenge to world democracy.

One of the most enduring—and frightening—images of recent years was the destruction by the Taliban of a centuries-old Buddhist shrine in Afghanistan. This was a wanton and barbaric act. It shows the kind of thing that can happen when fanatical religion merges with politics. It's impossible to imagine how any person could be free to seek God under such a regime.

Conclusion

As a Christian, I don't believe that God cares how man organizes himself politically. I base this on the experience of Jesus Christ, who was born a subject of the Roman Empire, a brutal, pagan regime. However, Christ never challenged Roman rule or even questioned it. In fact, on at least one occasion He ministered to a Roman soldier's servant;[4] He also recognized that the Roman Empire had legitimate claims on its subjects.[5] For their part, the Romans had no problem with

---

[4] Matthew 8:5–13.

[5] "Render therefore unto Caesar the things that are Caesar's and unto God the things that are God's" (Mark 12:17).

Christ, either. It wasn't until the Jewish leaders, fearing that Christ's teachings might undermine their authority, put pressure on Pontius Pilate, so that he reluctantly agreed to have Christ executed.

But Christ indicated no preference for one political system over another. His only concern was man's relationship with God.

I suppose it would be possible for a person to find God even under a repressive political system (some would go so far as to say that state persecution actually fosters religious conversion, as it did for Christianity during the early Roman Empire). A democratic society like ours, in spite of its excesses and distractions, does provide the opportunity for anyone to pursue God—or anything else. But this is precisely our dilemma: excessive freedom promotes excessive indulgence, so that even though man is free, he finds it extremely difficult to find God amid the sights, sounds, and sensations of contemporary life.

Still, given the choice, I think most religiously minded people would prefer a corrupting democracy to a stifling dictatorship.

Page 118, 1. 13: "This the" should read "This is the."

Page 156: The following text should be inserted:

9.   Religion

Mersault: [On death row] For the first time in months, I
thought about Mama. And now it seemed to me that
I understood why at her life's end she had taken a
fiancée, why she had pretended to make a new beginning. There, too, in that home where lives were
flickering out; there, too, dusk came as a mournful
solace. Being so close to death, Mama must have felt
a great release and ready to start all over again. No
one had the right to weep for her. And I too felt ready
to start life all over again. It was as if my great rush
of anger had washed me clean, purged me of all
hope; and gazing up at the night sky for the very first
time, I opened my heart to the sweet indifference of
the universe. And I felt that it was so much like myself, almost like a brother, that I realized that I had
been happy and that I was happy still.

—The Stranger[1]

_____

[1] This is the 1967 movie version of the Camus novel, starring Marcello
Mastroianni. It should not be confused with another movie of the same name
(1946), starring Orson Welles, Edward G. Robinson, and Loretta Young, about
a Nazi war criminal hiding in a small Connecticut town.

Background

My first truly intellectual pleasure was—geometry! Previously, in my freshman year of high school, I had an inkling that mathematics might be stimulating—even fun—when I encountered algebra. I was intrigued by the fact that, given three quantities, two of which were known, you could always determine the third. The only thing that prevented me from enjoying algebra was the teacher, who was undoubtedly the most terrifying figure I have ever met in a classroom—or anywhere else, for that matter. It was the only time in my education when the consequences for failing to grasp a subject were as severe as those for mischief or deceit. No consideration was given for effort. I saw a classmate get kicked in the pants merely for his inability to solve an equation on the blackboard. Physical fear cancelled any possibility of enjoying the subject.

My second-year mathematics teacher, Robert "Rockin' Bob" Barry, was about as different in manner and appearance from my algebra teacher as night is from day. A slender man of average height, he spoke in a continuous, suppressed monotone. This would have put us to sleep, except for his wry humor, which was worth staying awake for, not to mention the profound mathematical truths which he systematically laid before us. The chief of these was that, starting with a few self-evident propositions, you could construct an entire system of knowledge by a series of simple deductions.

It was not only beautiful but practical. I took to it like a fish to water and achieved a final grade of 100 percent. Not before or since have I been so completely in tune with a subject.

Using the methodology of geometry, I would like to make an attempt at formulating a religion, based on a few fundamental assumptions (which would be called postulates in geometry), which themselves are based on both observation and speculation, but which can be neither proved nor disproved. However, if you grant the validity of my assumptions, as well as the logic which accompanies them, I think you will find the results both compelling and—surprisingly—comforting!

Let's start with the existence of God. From a philosophical/scientific standpoint, I believe there are three possibilities:

1. There is no God, in the sense of a supreme, intelligent being.
2. God exists, but is uninterested in the world He created.
3. God exists, and He is a loving God.

I suppose, in order to cover all the logical possibilities, there could exist a malevolent God; but I don't see any sense in discussing such a case. Why would God create something only to demean or destroy it? Besides, such a scenario would be too depressing to contemplate.

Case 1: No God

One of my high school teachers, a Jesuit priest named John Lowe, once told us in the course of our sixth-period English class that it was impossible to prove the non-eternity of matter from reason. In other words, the material world may be eternal. It has always existed and will always exist. There is no need, therefore, to postulate the existence of a Creator. Eternity, like infinity, is a concept which is impossible for us to grasp; for our experience of existence is always in the context of change, separation, and causality. Even mathematics, the most abstract branch of science, and metaphysics, the study of *being* as such, are unable to explain these concepts. Perhaps the best we can do is to say that eternity is the opposite of time and that infinity is the opposite of space.

Our most basic understanding of time is in terms of change. Two days ago, the flower was in full bloom; now it has begun to wilt. There is always a before and an after. Nothing stays the same. Astronomers tell us that even the universe as a whole is evolving, not only in time but in space. It's actually getting bigger! It's impossible for us to conceive of something which simply *is:* unmoving, unchanging, where the terms before and after, here and there, have no meaning. Of course, change itself may be an eternal process, where matter continually rearranges its atoms and molecules in accordance with certain immutable laws. Without delving too deeply into science or philosophy, I think it's perfectly logical to say that a material world with no God is possible. However, such a world would have no meaning, in the sense of an ultimate purpose, unless we could understand and master the processes of matter so as to make the world and ourselves immortal. In such a case, it would make sense to develop an ethics whose sole purpose would be to extend and enhance the existence of the world and ourselves.

Theoretically, I don't see why this could not someday be possible: understanding the secret of life so that it could be prolonged indefinitely and the ability to control the behavior of the universe on the largest of scales, so that we would always have the necessary resources at our disposal. It seems like an enormous undertaking, but hopefully there would be sufficient time. After all, the sun should be stable for the next five billion years or so; and provided we don't incinerate the Earth or otherwise render it uninhabitable (or a rogue asteroid does the job for us), that should provide us the wherewithal, given the pace at which our knowledge has proceeded thus far (at least in the scientific and technological fields, if not the philosophical).

The only problem with such a scenario is that the person or persons who master the universe have no particular reason to share this knowledge and its benefits with others. They may decide to keep this to themselves, thereby letting everybody else die. Or, they may permit some people to exist and in effect become lord(s) over them. An ethics based purely on survival would probably resemble that of the Third Reich.

Case 2: An Indifferent God

The notion of an indifferent God goes back to the Deist philosophers of the 18th century. Isaac Newton in his *Principia Mathematica* had demonstrated that the world behaved according to laws which could be expressed mathematically. The motions of the planets, for example, could be explained by the Law of Gravitation. This represented, in the words of Thomas Kuhn,[2] a *paradigm shift:* a fundamental change in the way we look at things.

Philosophers and theologians, looking for a way to reconcile the new world view with traditional religious teach-

---

[2] *The Structure of Scientific Revolutions.*

ing, came up with the metaphor of the watchmaker and the watch. God, the watchmaker, created the world, symbolized by the watch. The watch, once made, functions in accordance with its material construction and its principles of design. Its operation is understandable and therefore predictable. Other than periodic winding and perhaps occasional maintenance, which can be performed by the user, the watch needs no further involvement of the maker. So, too, the world.

This fits in perfectly with Darwin's Theory of Evolution, which came along in the 19th century. As a complement to the basic rules governing the physical universe, discovered by Newton, Darwin had added an explanation of the origin and development of life.

To conservative religious thinkers, who insisted on a literal interpretation of the creation stories in the Bible, Darwin's ideas were a threat. More imaginative thinkers, like Pierre Teilhard de Chardin, incorporated Darwinian concepts into a new theology, which tried to take advantage of all the latest scientific discoveries in an attempt to provide a more comprehensive vision of man and his relation to the cosmos.

Getting back to Case 2. All of these scientific advances led to the idea that God might be detached from His creation. In other words, God has turned over the keys to us. Henceforth, we are on our own. While this idea might be attractive to some people, for a variety of reasons, I don't see that it is significantly different from Case 1. Perhaps the only difference is that, while giving us a free rein, God will ultimately not allow things to get out of hand. Perhaps, without being aware of it, we are acting under the illusion of free will; and all of our individual decisions will cumulatively result in a predetermined outcome.

Case 3: A Loving God

This is the one I prefer. I suspect that everybody else would, too; except that they may not have sufficient reasons to justify a belief that this is indeed the reality.

Allow me to express *my* reasons.

Let me begin with the observation that there is a general discrediting of religion today, especially in the West. This is nothing new. It is a process which began with Copernicus and reached its philosophical culmination with Nietzsche. In historical terms, there are three defining events or movements which have led people to question the desirability of religious commitment: (1) Christian Fundamentalism, (2) Islamic Fundamentalism, and (3) the Holocaust. Let me discuss each of these in turn.

Christian Fundamentalism is a reaction to the growing coarseness and self-centeredness of Western civilization, best expressed by the phrase *secular humanism.* Robert Bork, William Bennett, and others have attacked this tendency on philosophical and utilitarian grounds. But for many others who are distressed at the apparent decline, if not abandonment, of traditional Christian values in our public and private behavior, the response has been the adoption of a total and uncritical acceptance of the Bible as a guide to human conduct. This has led to an ugly confrontation between religious conservatives and so-called "cultural elitists" over such diverse issues as gay rights, abortion, and pornography. It has become an all-out, no-holds-barred struggle in which neither side is willing to compromise or at least seek common ground. It has led to a political divide in the United States, the intensity of which has not been seen since the civil rights and antiwar movements of the 1960s. The result is a polarization of American society in which anyone who professes "traditional" moral values is branded as a religious fanatic, while anyone who insists on equal rights for gays is demonized as a godless liberal. In the culture wars, as in shooting wars, truth is always the first casualty.

The sad result of all this is that any kind of religious inquiry, philosophical or otherwise, is deemed anti-intellectual and therefore avoided, at least in public.

Religion has also been discredited by Islamic Fundamentalism. The destructive effects of extreme religious views, culminating in 9/11, have caused many people to fear religion, even loathe it. In many circles, religion is regarded as the chief obstacle to human progress.

But the one human experience, perhaps more than any other, which has caused people to doubt, even deny, the existence of God is the Holocaust. The question is: How could God permit the mass murder of innocents? The answer to this seemingly simple question is complex. Let me begin with a philosophical/historical perspective.

Postulate 1: *Existential Equivalence*

As I stated earlier, I will attempt to formulate a religion based on some fundamental assumptions or postulates. The first of these I will call *existential equivalence.* Basically, this means that there is no privileged position in time or space.

Existential equivalence is analogous to the *cosmological principle* in astronomy, which states that there is no preferred place in the universe; i.e., the overall features of the universe will look the same no matter where you are located in the universe. In other words, an astronomer on a planet in a solar system in a faraway galaxy would look in our direction and come to the same conclusions about the origin and properties of the universe as we would.

The principle of existential equivalence implies that:

1. Man's nature is the same throughout his existence on this planet.
2. As a consequence, the meaning of man's existence is, has been, and will be the same.
3. Environmental changes, scientific and technological advancements, etc. are essentially irrelevant to man's unique mode of existence, which is in the realm of moral choice.
4. This principle can only be rendered invalid by a change in man's nature; e.g., by his becoming immortal.

I believe that the principle of existential equivalence can help us make sense of man's most terrible collective experience: the Holocaust.

In one sense, the Holocaust was nothing new. It was certainly not the first time that one group of people have tried to exterminate another group simply because of *who they were.* The Romans persecuted the Christians, the Christians attacked the Moslems, the Russians starved the Ukrainians, etc., etc. The Holocaust was unique only in its scale and mode of execution. With typical efficiency and thoroughness, the Nazis converted genocide into an industrial process. They found a new application for the techniques of mass production. It was the perfect confluence of ideology, technology, and industrial engineering.

Perhaps the most difficult thing about the Holocaust for us to accept is the overwhelming sense of injustice and cruelty that it represents. We are haunted by the cries of innocent children being coldly and systematically murdered, as though they were nothing more than insects being removed by an exterminator.

And yet, as Camus said, we are all under sentence of death. Ontologically, what is the difference between the prisoner awaiting execution on death row and the rest of us? We were thrust into our earthly existence without our knowledge or consent. There is no escape, save death. The only difference between the prisoner on death row and the rest of humanity is that the prisoner is probably more certain as to the time of his death and that, in the meantime, he has considerably less freedom of movement. To paraphrase Evel Knievel, the great motorcycle daredevil: "All of us are headed toward death; the only difference is, I'll probably get there sooner!"

Postulate 2: *Made for Each Other*

In the first chapter of his *Confessions,* Saint Augustine writes:

. . . you [God] have made us for yourself, and our hearts are restless until they can find peace in you.[3]

In other words, there is in man an irreducible element,

---

[3] *The Confessions of St. Augustine,* translated by Rex Warner (New York, Mentor-Omega Books, 1963), p. 17.

traditionally called "the soul," which is eternal, like God Himself. The soul transcends even consciousness, which psychic researchers are trying to explain as patterns of neurons firing in the brain. Perhaps this is so, perhaps not. Or perhaps the very idea of a spirit-matter distinction is artificial and unnecessary, since matter itself may have a spiritual as well as material aspect, analogous to the particle-wave duality of light.

The bottom line is that the world we are most familiar with, the world of money, power, sex, etc., cannot truly satisfy man. This world can provide distractions and diversions, things which can give us the illusion of meaning and fulfillment. But only God can satisfy our souls. Speaking from personal experience, I can attest that this is true. At least I have found nothing thus far which I can say has truly satisfied me; and I have tried many things—all that I have cared to—though I can't say that I have found God, either. But there have been times (e.g., in my epiphanies—see Chapter 3), when I've had an inkling that there was something or someone just beyond my five senses. Perhaps this is man's mission: to find God amidst the noise and confusion of life.

How does one go about doing this? Maybe by using the world as a means and not an end. Seen from this perspective, the world may not be a distraction or diversion, but rather a roadmap to God. This can work on many levels. All one has to do is look around to be amazed at the incredible complexity of the world: how living organisms from amoebas to man have evolved from basic matter; how the solutions to all man's material needs are available in nature; how man himself has accomplished wondrous deeds, from art to philosophy to science.

166

In the chapter entitled "Living," I contend that there are three fundamentally worthwhile things one can do in this life. They are:

- Knowing
- Creating
- Loving

To me, these represent the pinnacle of living a meaningful life (without resorting to religious concepts such as the soul or a Supreme Being). Many people who are fortunate enough to have experienced any or all of them may not wish to go any farther, figuring perhaps that this is the highest level they can aspire to. However, each of the above activities can lead to an encounter with God. Take knowledge, for example. The more we know, the more we appreciate what we don't know. The deeper science probes the workings of nature, the more questions arise. Perhaps at some point we'll hit a blank wall. In cosmology, we may be approaching the limits of what is knowable. What goes on inside a black hole? Apparently, our present understanding of science, the basic structure of which is represented by the General Theory of Relativity (on the macrocosmic scale) and the Quantum Theory (on the microcosmic scale), breaks down when we cross the event horizon of these cosmic vacuum cleaners. The Big Bang Theory, which is our best explanation of the origin of the universe, can't actually take us back to the moment of creation, let alone "before," since "before" and "after" are concepts relating to time, which was itself created, along with space, in the Big Bang! At the edges of human knowledge, therefore, we may take a leap of faith to God; or, even better, our knowledge may transform itself into wisdom, in which case we may be permitted to know the mind of God.

The creative process is by definition a godlike endeavor. Those who experience the joy and power of bringing something—or someone—into being must surely have some notion of God.

And then there is love, perhaps the best way to God. The Gospels say that God so loved the world that He sent his only Son, Jesus Christ, to redeem it and sanctify it. Traditional Christian theology says that the Holy Spirit, the mysterious Third Person of the Blessed Trinity, is actually the love of God the Father for His Son. In short, God *is* love. Any person who experiences human love in its purest and most disinterested form must certainly know what God is like.

Postulate 3: *All Religions Converge in God*

All the world's religions, both great and small, have emerged in their particular circumstances of time and place. Some, such as Judaism, are identified with the historical destiny of a nation or people; others, such as Christianity, claim to have a universal application. I believe that whatever their origin, they all end up in the same place: the Indescribable, the Ineffable, the Mystery. The Person encountered by Thomas Merton is the One encountered by Gandhi.

Theology, which Saint Augustine defined as faith seeking understanding, is an attempt to codify, delineate, and elucidate what is essentially a personal encounter between God and man. Moses and the Ten Commandments are perhaps the best known example of this. Scholars and theologians are still debating the ramifications of that meeting. However, no theological system, regardless of its erudition and complexity, can adequately describe or encompass a religious experience. Perhaps each of the world's religions can be traced back to such an event, in which the founder met God. Here are a few examples:

- Judaism: Abraham at Canaan; Moses at Mt. Sinai
- Islam: Muhammad in the cave at Mt. Hira
- Buddhism: Siddhartha Gauthama under the pipal tree at Bodh Gaya
- Christianity: Jesus Christ at the River Jordan
- Mormonism: Joseph Smith at Hill Cumorah, near Palmyra, New York

As an example of the convergence of theological thought in widely divergent religions, consider the Christian doctrine of Purgatory and the Hindu doctrine of Reincarnation. The unifying idea in both these doctrines is that the human soul must be purified of all sins, imperfections, and worldly attachments before it can be united with God. In Christian theology, this purification is accomplished in Purgatory, which is a transitional state between the eternal opposites of heaven and hell. Here, by some unknown process (which could be reincarnation, as in Hinduism), the soul is cleansed before being admitted to heaven. In the Hindu doctrine of reincarnation, the human soul, after the death of its earthly body, reenters the world in another body, which may be either animal or human, depending on the level of purity attained in its former life.

169

Postulate 4: *Life Is the Medium of Our Becoming*

What this means, essentially, is that life is not an end in itself, but a means to an end. And what is that end? Self-definition. In other words, life is to man what water is to the fish: an environment in which to become what one is capable of becoming.

Becoming, however, is not the same as accomplishing, which is generally regarded as the best way to judge the worth of a person's life. What has he or she *done*? How much money has he made? How many books has she written? How many sick people has he cured?

Becoming, on the other hand, is the process of intellectual and spiritual growth, culminating in the attainment of wisdom, which can best be described as seeing the world as God sees it; i.e., from the standpoint of eternity. From this perspective, what happens in the world is not as important as how we look at it.

To the extent that events in the world are the result of human agency, the prime motivating factor is insecurity. This in turn produces fear, which then leads to a whole range of actions, chief among which are the pursuit of money, the obsession with health and safety, and aggressive behavior, both individually and collectively. The preoccupations of insecurity preempt man's nobler instincts, such as compassion. If wisdom can be said to have a practical effect, it is the elimination of insecurity. This allows for a certain detachment from the world (*not indifference*—see footnote on page 131), because with detachment comes the assurance that God ultimately has things under control.

One of my fondest recollections of my high school

teaching career is of the day I was sitting next to Edith Sullivan in the teachers' lunch room, feeling depressed and despondent at my inability to handle disruptive students in my ninth grade English class. Judging by Edith's demeanor, you would not have suspected that she was having the same problems—and worse—that I was. On top of that, she was laboring under several handicaps that I didn't have:

- She was frail-looking and small (no more than a hundred pounds).
- She was a black person in an almost all-white school.
- She had a heavy Jamaican accent which even I, a linguist by inclination, had difficulty sometimes understanding.

But there was an inscrutable calmness about her, as though she were looking down upon the scene from a great height. On this particular day, I was more disturbed than usual. Although I prided myself on not being a whiner or complainer, I unloaded my frustrations on Edith. After listening impassively to my woes, she said simply: "Even the Master did not succeed."

Taken aback by this cryptic remark, I asked her what she meant. She explained:

Jesus Christ, Son of God, Second Person of the Blessed Trinity, Lord of Creation, chose to be born among us. He came to proclaim the Kingdom of God. Both Master of the Universe and spiritual Master, he nevertheless failed to complete the project He began: the triumph and reign of the Kingdom. Therefore, why should *we* feel discouraged, when God Himself did not finish the job? It would be presumptive indeed for us to think that we could or should do what the Master did not. Rather, we should be content to do what we can, even if it appears insignificant, knowing that God will ultimately bring all to fruition in His own time.

By all accounts she took her own advice.

If detachment is the consequence of wisdom, does the wise man eschew involvement in the world and its evils, preferring instead to remain on the sidelines by, for example, going off to a monastery or retiring to a wilderness retreat?

Not necessarily.

It has been said (by Camus, I think, among others) that the ultimate freedom of man consists in his ability to choose an attitude in the face of whatever fate confronts him. This freedom is available to man regardless of his circumstances. In answer to the above question, let me make two assertions:

- There will always be a place for the purely contemplative person, even if that person has no direct connection with the world. In *Lost Horizon,* Fr. Pero tells Conway that the mission of Shangri-La is to protect and preserve the noblest accomplishments of man, following the path of moderation in all things.
- If a person chooses to become involved in battling the evils of the world, he must be careful not to become dehumanized in the heat of the struggle.

As to the second point, let me provide two examples, one positive and one negative.

No one can doubt the passion and purity of Jesus Christ, to whom sin was anathema. Despite His commitment to eradicate evil, He "never lost His cool" when confronted with it (except perhaps the time He chased the moneychangers from the Temple, which was perhaps a symbolic and not a real act of violence). He never succumbed to the perfectly natural and human temptation to exact revenge. But He was always uncompromising in His exposure and condemnation of evil. He allowed Himself to be tortured and crucified, even though He had the power to destroy His tormentors. Nevertheless, He started a revolution which continues to this day, by appealing to man's best self. In the words of the Beatles:

> You say you want a revolution, but you've got to change your mind instead.

On the negative side, take the case of the man who, in the name of protecting the unborn, murdered a doctor who performed abortions. A clear example of two wrongs don't make a right. The good news is that neither the abortionist nor his victims, ultimately, will be deprived of life.

Which brings us to the next postulate.

Postulate 5: *The Conservation of Life*

Analogous to the principle of energy conservation in science, also called the First Law of Thermodynamics, is the principle of life conservation in religion, which prevents man from definitively destroying life.

The Law of the Conservation of Energy states that the sum total of all the matter and energy[4] in the universe is constant. In other words, matter/energy can neither be created nor de-

---

[4] According to Einstein's famous $E=mc^2$, matter and energy are interchangeable.

stroyed—*only transformed.* Life, therefore, which is part of the matter-energy continuum, can neither be created nor destroyed. But like everything else we see around us, life can change, both in appearance and substance. The laws of chemistry govern the ordinary transformations of matter from one form to another. The laws of nuclear physics (quantum mechanics, to be exact) govern the transformation of matter into energy or vice versa. When a living organism dies, it does not cease to exist—it merely changes state. Perhaps the thing that makes something alive—the life-force, if you will—is just a form of energy.

So, in a very real sense, man is incapable of committing murder—or destroying any of God's creatures.

Postulate 6: *No Progress— Time's Arrow Notwithstanding*

In 1944, the poet e.e. cummings wrote:

pity this busy monster, manunkind,

not. Progress is a comfortable disease:[5]

And this:

—when skies are hanged and oceans drowned,
the single secret will still be man[6]

One of the great unresolved questions in science is The

---

[5] e. e. cummings: *POEMS 1923–1954* (New York, Harcourt, Brace & World, Inc., 1968), p. 397.
[6] Ibid, p. 401.

Arrow of Time: the distinction between the past and the future. The problem is this:

> At the subatomic level, neither the old ideas of classical mechanics nor the modern theory of quantum mechanics distinguish between the past and the future. In a typical interaction involving subatomic particles, two particles may come together and interact in some way to produce two different particles, which then separate. The laws of physics say that almost every such interaction can run equally well in reverse . . .
>
> But at the macroscopic level of our human senses, the distinction between the past and future is obvious. Things wear out; people get older. In the equivalent of the particle reaction, we can imagine a wine glass balanced precariously on the edge of a table, then falling to the floor and smashing. We never see smashed glasses reassembling themselves, even though every interaction involving the atoms of the wine glass as it smashes is, according to the known laws of physics, reversible.[7]

Without going into a discussion of this question, about which entire books have been written without any definitive resolution (cf., for example, *The Arrow of Time*[8]), it's fascinating to think that at the most fundamental level of existence, there is no past or future, only—what? The eternal present?

Ever since Lyell on the geological level, Darwin on the biological level, and Hubble on the astrophysical level, we

---

[7] John Gribbin, *Companion to the Cosmos* (New York, Little, Brown and Company, 1996), p. 29.

[8] Peter Coveney and Roger Highfield, *The Arrow of Time* (New York, Fawcett Columbine, 1990).

have been confronted with the idea of an evolving universe. This naturally leads to the question of whether evolution is evident in human history as well. In Judaeo-Christian theology, this is a central theme: God's intervention at decisive moments in history to influence the course of events in a certain direction. Several of these events are:

- Man's creation—Adam and Eve
- The Great Flood—Noah and the Ark
- The Call of Abraham
- The Ten Commandments—Moses
- The Incarnation—Christ's birth
- The Resurrection—Christ's rising from the dead
- The Second Coming

A related question is whether and to what extent Man is to play a part in this cosmic drama. This is a question I posed at the beginning of this essay and is of critical importance in answering the two most basic questions of all; namely:

- What is the meaning of existence in general?
- What is the meaning of *my* existence?

If indeed there is such a thing as historical evolution, is it the determining factor in the final disposition of creation? In other words, are we building something permanent here? If so, then everything we do here is of the utmost importance, since our future depends on it.

The problem I have with this line of reasoning is the fact that the world is replete with failure, inequality, and injustice, both in the present and in the past. How do we account for all the people who have gotten a raw deal, mostly through no fault of their own? What about the people who are born crippled or with incurable diseases? What about the people, many of them children, who were murdered in the Holocaust? And the victims of terror attacks?

If God is Love, as we have been assuming in the course of this discussion, then it would be inconceivable for Him to construct a world where these things can happen, *unless it didn't matter what happened.* Ideas such as time's arrow, evolution, and progress may be significant only in the development of our individual souls—our spiritual persona—not in the overall scheme of things, which rests solely with God.

And so, I reiterate the conclusion I arrived at earlier: our purpose in life is to follow the direction of our spiritual hunger—our restlessness of soul—and discover God.

It is only by discovering and loving God that we can become capable of exerting a positive influence on the world around us. In theological terms, this is holiness—or the state of grace—or salvation. Many people try to attain this condition by doing good works. In a way, it goes back to the Puritan notion, still very influential in the United States, that what a person accomplishes, both materially and morally, is a reliable indicator of his spiritual status: i.e., whether he is saved or not. This is equivalent to the idea of buying your way into heaven, as wealthy people in the Catholic Church used to try to do with plenary indulgences.[9] It is also related to the idea that we can alter or influence events by prayer, as if we had to cajole a stubborn or lazy God into action.

---

[9] An indulgence was the process of having your sins forgiven by making a monetary donation to the Church. A plenary indulgence, which could be merited by a more generous contribution, guaranteed even greater forgiveness.

However, I think that spiritual efficacy in the world, to the extent that it is the result of human effort, really works in the opposite way: i.e., that knowing God fills us to overflowing with His love, so that it spills over into our attitude toward His creation, manifesting itself in unselfishness and generosity. Herein the self finds its true identity.

So how does one find God? By looking:

"Seek and you shall find."

Conclusion

This chapter began with the goal of trying to construct a religion by following the methodology of geometry: start with a few self-evident propositions or postulates and then draw conclusions by simple deduction, using those conclusions in turn to draw further conclusions, and so on down the line. Although the postulates laid down may appear to be "non-denominational," so to speak, the reader has undoubtedly noticed that much of the subsequent discussion has been heavily influenced by my particular religious heritage: Roman Catholic Christianity.[10] I make no apology for this. All I can offer by way of defense or explanation is that Christianity, as it was revealed to me by the Jesuits, has always seemed to have a universal application. What started as a branch of

---

[10] I might add the word "Jesuit" in front of this, since my brand of Catholicism has been heavily influenced by my formal Jesuit education and particularly by my association with individual Jesuits.

178

Judaism, where ethnicity and religion were inextricably entwined, became, at a critical moment,[11] a new religion, where everyone was welcome, regardless of their heritage.

A close reading of the Gospels indicates that Christ, Himself a devout Jew, nevertheless invited everyone into the Kingdom: Jews, Samaritans, even the hated Romans. This universality was underlined by the missionary journeys of St. Paul, who roamed the ancient world, proclaiming the Kingdom to the citizens of Ephesus, Corinth, and Thessalonica, among others.

For 2,000 years, Christianity has provided the ethical underpinnings for Western Civilization, although, as Chesterton observed:

> The Christian ideal has not been tried and found wanting. It has been found difficult; and left untried.[12]

And not just the West. Gandhi, long before he became known as the Mahatma, founded his ethical teachings on the Gospels. The United Nations, as the League of Nations before it, operates on generally accepted Christian principles, as when it tries to arbitrate international disputes or provide disaster relief. After all, it's pretty hard to deny the depth and breadth of the following statements:

> And one of the Scribes came forward . . . and . . . asked him which was the first commandment of all. But Jesus answered

---

[11] Symbolized by the confrontation between St. Peter and St. Paul over the question of whether the movement initiated by Jesus Christ was to remain in Judaism.

[12] G.K. Chesterton, *What's Wrong with the World* (London, 1910), Part 1, Chapter 5.

him, "The first commandment of all is, 'Hear, O Israel! The Lord our God is one God; and thou shalt love the Lord thy God with thy whole heart, and with thy whole soul, and with thy whole mind, and with thy whole strength.' This is the first commandment. And the second is like it, 'Thou shalt love thy neighbor as thyself.' There is no other commandment greater than these."[13]

Whole volumes of theology are contained in the above passage. For now, I would just like to make a few points:

- God is One and the Same, whether you are a Buddhist, a Christian, a Hindu, a Jew, a Moslem, a Taoist, or whatever.
- Loving God makes it possible to love our fellow man.
- Loving God involves every aspect of the self:

  —Heart (emotions)
  —Soul (spirit)
  —Mind (intellect)
  —Strength (will)

- The second commandment is a concise version of the Golden Rule ("Do unto others as you would have them do unto you").

This may be a stretch, but I find it interesting that Christ used the word "neighbor" when speaking about the love we should have for each other. Some, perhaps most, theologians have extended the concept of "neighbor" to include everyone else

---

[13] Mark 12:28–31.

in the world. This is undoubtedly true, but I wonder if Christ had something else in mind as well. Perhaps He chose the word "neighbor" because it indicates someone who is close to us, either geographically or emotionally. Perhaps He used "neighbor" in the sense of the phrase "Charity begins at home." One of my favorite scenes in the movie *The Hospital,* Paddy Chayefsky's dark comedy about the American health care system, is when Dr. Bock, brilliantly played by George C. Scott, bitterly complains to Miss Drummond (Diana Rigg) about his son:

> We had a son, 23 years old. I threw him out of the house last year. The sadistic little humbug. He preached universal love, and he despised everyone. He had a blanket contempt for the middle class, even its decencies. He detested my mother because she had a petit-bourgeoise pride in her son, the doctor. [Snickers.] I cannot tell you how brutishly he ignored that rather good lady. When she died, he didn't even come to the funeral. He felt the chapel service was a hypocrisy. He told me his generation didn't live with lies. I said, listen, everybody lives with lies. [Laughs.] I grabbed him by his poncho, and I dragged him the length of our seven-room, despicably affluent, middle-class apartment, and I flung him—out! Haven't seen him since.

What an apt summation of the radical 60s! So much abominable behavior disguised as idealism and love. Ironically, the "greatest generation"[14] had collectively spawned a monster.

---

[14] This is a reference to the title of a book by Tom Brokaw, *The Greatest Generation* (New York, Random House, 1998), in which he talks about the men and women who experienced both The Great Depression and World War II, who were the parents of the generation which came of age in the 1960s.

Thus, you have my conception of a universal religion, with its decidedly Catholic Christian bias. From what I know of other religions, it is not something which would be uncomfortable for any person of any faith. The ethical principles implied in such a religion are almost universally accepted. As for God, no one really knows. The various ideas about God propounded by the major religions are to my mind not incompatible. In fact, they are complementary. For no single system is big enough to encompass the Almighty, Who must remain a Mystery—to be fully apprehended, perhaps, only after we die. Which brings us full circle[15] back to the title of this book.

---

[15] The circle is often used as a symbol for God because it has no beginning and no end.

Conclusion

Pia: Father! Oh, Father!

Bishop: What is it, child?

Pia: Here [handing the Bishop a letter explaining her "miracle"].

Bishop: There *was* a miracle, Pia. You see, child, the things of God that are marvelous are to be believed in. But sometimes reason destroys, because it proves to the reasoning mind only that which is reasonable and it leaves out all that is marvelous. But all is well, child, all will be well. The miracle was in your own faith. Keep that faith, my dear, keep it always, with God's everlasting blessing.

                                 —*Quick Let's Get Married*

Or, as Pascal said:

The heart has its reasons which the reason does not know.[1]

    And so we return to the two questions posed at the beginning:

---

[1] *Pensees,* No. 277.

1. What is the meaning of life in general?
2. What is the meaning of *my* life?

Based on the reflections of the previous chapters, I will attempt to provide an answer (at least a tentative one) to each of them.

What is the Meaning of Life in General?

The purpose of life in general (i.e., for *all* of us and for *all* of creation) is to *find God*. As the Jesuit philosopher and scientist Pierre Teilhard de Chardin argued, the entire universe, culminating in man, is evolving toward God.[2] In the Gospel of St. John (12: 32), Christ declares:

And I, if I be lifted up from the earth, will draw all things to myself.

As I have tried to point out in the various chapters, there is nothing in this life[3] which can truly satisfy man. Speaking for myself, I have not found anything which has satisfied me—and I've tried a lot of things. On the other hand, there is

---

[2] Teilhard calls this rendezvous of God and creation the Omega Point. This is a reference to God's famous saying in the Bible "I am the alpha [beginning] and the omega [end]." Alpha (α) and omega (ω) are the first and last letters of the ancient Greek alphabet.

[3] By "this life" I mean the familiar world of material things (money, possessions, bodily pleasures, etc.), as well as the usual motivating forces, such as ambition, fame, power, etc.

ample testimony from around the world and from history that those who have encountered God have achieved fulfillment. They have no need to look any further for meaning or purpose.

What is the Meaning of *My* Life?

While finding God is our common destiny, each one of us has an individual destiny that is unique. In other words, our individuality will be preserved for eternity. Life provides us with the opportunity to develop in our own peculiar way.

Our uniqueness, aside from our DNA, consists in *how we find God.* This is what provides us with the unique meaning of our lives, for each of us must find God differently, according to our own circumstances, personality, talents, etc.

Even those whose life has been cut short (e.g., children murdered in the Holocaust or aborted fetuses) have a unique identity, though it may only be their DNA.[4]

Perhaps our *experience* of God will be unique, too.

---

[4] Every human being who has ever existed or will exist on this planet has a unique DNA, *formed at the moment of conception.* The only exceptions to this are (1) a clone—an individual which is a genetic copy of another, artificially produced and (2) identical twins. However, as the evil Doctor Mengele in *The Boys from Brazil* found out, clones don't become identical people, even when placed in similar environments.

Synthesis

In the Introduction, and throughout the rest of this book, I have considered the question of life's meaning as two separate inquiries (the meaning of life in general and the meaning of *my* life). However, as can be seen from the above paragraphs and all that has gone before, the two meanings ultimately merge in the quest for God. What makes my life different from any other is only the *way* in which I find God. The end result (i.e., God) is the same for everyone; the difference is how we get there.

As the German theologian Paul Tillich said, faith is a matter of ultimate concern. This means that God must be the most important thing in our lives, the thing we are most concerned about.

This is my faith, and this is my hope. Only in death will I know for sure.